BRITAIN, THE SIX-DAY WAR
AND ITS AFTERMATH

FRANK BRENCHLEY

I.B. TAURIS

LONDON · NEW YORK

Published in 2005 by I.B.Tauris & Co. Ltd
6 Salem Road, London W2 4BU
175 Fifth Avenue, New York, NY 10010
www.ibtauris.com

In the United States of America and Canada distributed by Palgrave Mac-
millan, a division of St Martin's Press, 175 Fifth Avenue, New York, NY
10010

International Library of Twentieth-Century History 3

ISBN: 1 85043 406 9
EAN: 978 1 85043 406 1

A full CIP record for this book is available from the British Library
A full CIP record for this book is available from the Library of Congress

Library of Congress catalog card: available

Typeset in Bliss by A. & D. Worthington, Newmarket, Suffolk
Printed and bound in Great Britain by TJ International Ltd, Padstow, Cornwall

CONTENTS

ACKNOWLEDGEMENTS

MY THANKS ARE DUE to the staff of the Public Record Office; the librarians of the Bodleian Library and the Library of the Middle East Centre of St Antony's College, Oxford; to the Archivist of the LBJ Library in Austin, Texas; to Professor Avi Shlaim, who lent me valuable secondary sources; and most especially to Professor James Piscatori, who supervised the production of my doctoral thesis on this subject. I am also grateful to the Warden and Fellows of Merton College, Oxford, who sanctioned my membership of the college during the three years of study which were the foundation of this book. They were, I think, amused that, for the first time in the over 700 years of the college's existence, they had a Fellow who was simultaneously a graduate student.

NOTE ON SOURCES

THE PRINCIPAL BRITISH PRIMARY SOURCES used in the writing of this book were the Public Record Office papers for 1967–68. Files consulted were mainly in the categories PREM, CAB, FCO and DEFE. Harold Wilson's papers are in the Bodleian Library but at the time of writing were not yet open. George Brown's papers are also in the Bodleian and are open (with the permission of his daughter, for which I am grateful), but contain little of interest for this book. Gore-Booth's papers in the Bodleian are also unproductive. The archival material was supplemented by interviews, especially with Denis Healey and George Thomson. These were useful but produced no sight of papers on relevant subjects, which neither of them had kept.

Foreign primary sources consulted were the printed United Nations documents; public papers of Presidents Eisenhower and Johnson; papers in the Foreign Relations of the United States series, plus a collection entitled *The Quest for Peace*; and the Israeli series, *Israeli Foreign Relations*. Arab countries concerned do not regularly open their archives, but some documents are annexed to secondary sources, particularly Heikal's *1967 – Al Infijar*.

There are a great number of memoirs published in English by persons involved in the events described, which are of considerable importance. Many other secondary sources are available, written mainly by British, American, Arab and Israeli authors, which contain some factual material and a wealth of analysis. Those consulted were for the most part in English, plus a few in Arabic. Journals of interest were the *Middle East Journal*, the *Journal of Palestine Studies* and *Foreign Affairs*. Use was also made of the BBC Monitoring Service for Arab and Israeli broadcasts (published in English translation). Newspapers were consulted in the British Library's newspaper library.

ABBREVIATIONS

CAB	Cabinet
CC	Cabinet Conclusions
DEFE	Defence
FCO	Foreign and Commonwealth Office
FO	Foreign Office
GAOR	General Assembly Official Record
PLO	Palestine Liberation Organization
PREM	Premier (Prime Minister)
PRO	Public Record Office
SCOR	Security Council Official Record
SOSFA	Secretary of State for Foreign Affairs
UAR	United Arab Republic (Egypt)
UKMIS	United Kingdom Mission
UN	United Nations
UNEF	United Nations Emergency Force
UNGA	United Nations General Assembly
UNTSO	United Nations Truce Supervisory Organization
UNWRA	United Nations Relief and Works Agency for Palestine Refugees

THE MAKING OF FOREIGN POLICY IN BRITAIN

IN 1975 WILLIAM WALLACE COMMENTED: 'The study of the process of making British foreign policy has until recently been neglected, disowned by most students of domestic politics, distantly acknowledged by scholars of international relations.'[1] Earlier David Vital had said: 'The literature on this subject is still very sparse; it is also random in its coverage and uneven in its quality. Official sources are extremely limited. ... It might ... be argued that ... only an insider who has participated personally in the processes described here over a long period should attempt a discussion of them.'[2] As I fit this formula, it seems appropriate for me to describe briefly the governmental background to the taking of the British policy decisions relevant to the following chapters. My description will apply particularly to the years 1967–68, when I was assistant under-secretary of state for Middle East affairs in the Foreign Office (later Foreign and Commonwealth Office), but will also draw on my experience as a deputy under-secretary of state in the Cabinet Office in 1975–76.

Machinery of government

The supreme control over British foreign policy, including policy towards the Middle East, lies of course with the cabinet. As Vital says: 'In law, no less than in fact, the conduct of Britain's foreign affairs is the peculiar concern and undivided responsibility of the Executive – a Crown prerogative. ... In ultimate terms the Cabinet is the Executive.'[3] Apart from consideration of cabinet papers tabled by the foreign secretary (who in 1967 was George Brown and after 15 March 1968 Michael Stewart), there was always opportunity for oral discussion of policy at the routine weekly cabinet meetings, where foreign affairs normally stood second on the agenda. In addition, there was a senior cabinet committee, the Defence and Oversea Policy Committee,[4] chaired by the prime minister (Harold Wilson in 1967–68), charged with responsibility for this subject. It had a smaller membership than the full cabinet, so was more discreet and was the normal arena for initial discussion of secret matters. Sometimes these matters might later be put before the full cabinet. This happened especially if they were of major policy importance or if they were likely to be controversial within the cabinet. In the latter case, they might need discussion before the full body, so that the conclusion should be binding on all its members under the rule of cabinet solidarity.

In 1967, presumably because the risk of an Arab–Israeli war was clearly a very important consideration and because different ministers had differing partialities for the two sides in the conflict, more use was made than usual of full cabinet proceedings on the subject. Nevertheless Wallace remarks:

> Some of the foreign policy problems faced by the Labour Government of 1964–70 were 'so to speak, blown on to the Cabinet by their suddenness and importance',[5] without the opportunity for full official discussion or the preparation of papers, sometimes without even a formal Cabinet agenda. Such were the lengthy discussions on whether or how to intervene in the Gulf of Aqaba in the hope of preventing war in the Middle East in June 1967.[6]

It may be worth adding here a comment about the records of cabinet discussions. These are not minutes in the usual sense of that word, but are called 'Cabinet Conclusions', abbreviated to 'CC' in their reference numbers. The secretary of the cabinet sits on the immediate right of the prime minister at cabinet meetings and takes such notes of the proceedings as he wishes. At the foot of the table sits the deputy secretary concerned with the subject under discussion, who takes a fuller account of statements and speakers. After the meeting, the deputy secretary dictates a short record of what was said, drawing on his full notes, and sends it to the cabinet secretary. The latter edits the various short records he has received from his several deputy secretaries and consolidates them into a single document, which he circulates on his own authority as the Cabinet Conclusions. There is no sight of this document by any minister before it is issued. This is contrary to the suspicion of several cabinet ministers, who in the case of Harold Wilson's cabinet firmly believed that the records were shown to and doctored by the prime minister. A similar procedure occurs with meetings of the Defence and Oversea Policy Committee, except that, in their case, the deputy secretary circulates the record, normally without sight of it by the cabinet secretary.

The record is of the conclusions reached by the cabinet or committee, preceded by enough of the discussion, with the principal arguments on both sides, to allow the reader to understand how those conclusions were reached. Normally the arguments are not attributed to particular speakers.[7] This is again a reflection of the principle of cabinet solidarity: the conclusions are those of the cabinet or the committee as a whole, and it could be disadvantageous to put on record which member put forward which argument. Cabinet Conclusions (at whatever time the cabinet is held) must be circulated in time to be with Whitehall departments by the beginning of the next morning's working session.

Attitudes of ministers

The relationship between the prime minister and the foreign secretary in the control of policy on foreign affairs varies a good deal from one administration to another. If the prime minister has himself been foreign secretary earlier in his career, as happened, for example, in the case of Anthony Eden, there is a likelihood that No. 10 Downing Street will exercise a possibly disproportionate influence over foreign policy matters, or attempt to do so. I remember, for instance, that at that time the career diplomat who was on the prime minister's staff as an assistant private secretary would often directly telephone a member whom he knew of the staff of a Foreign Office department to enquire what the Office was doing about a particular problem, rather than address his enquiry to the foreign secretary's private secretary. (The Prime Minister's Office receives advance copies of all telegrams of importance passing through the Foreign Office communications system, so knows what matters are afoot. The assistant private secretary from the Foreign Office at No. 10 is normally of first secretary or counsellor rank, so relatively junior, but naturally selected as an extremely able officer, who is likely to rise high in the Service.)

The case of Eden's premiership was, however, unusual at the time. As Vital points out, 'It is more than a coincidence that not one of the ten Prime Ministers between Lord Salisbury (1895–1902) and Sir Anthony Eden (1955–57) had been a foreign secretary prior to his premiership.'[8] Harold Wilson had never served in the Foreign Office and was generally more interested in domestic policy and party control than in foreign policy. There were one or two exceptions to this, however. Wilson longed to play a personal role in mediation on the Vietnam issue (a cause of differences between the United Kingdom and the United States, resulting from Britain's unwillingness to contribute forces to the Vietnam War, although some Commonwealth countries were doing so).[9] He also insisted on negotiating personally with Ian Smith on the Rhodesia problem, though he never succeeded in bringing such negotiations to a satisfactory conclusion.[10] However, he normally did not try to take a lead on Middle East issues, especially when George Brown was foreign secretary.

Their relationship was a delicate one. For instance, Brown did not like in conversation with his officials to use the phrase 'the prime minister'; he usually preferred 'my senior colleague'. As Wallace says: 'The difficulties of a situation in which an activist Prime

Minister and an energetic Foreign Secretary do not share a common outlook or a mutual understanding were well illustrated during George Brown's tenure of the Foreign Office.'[11]

However, this particular problem was not apparent during the May–June 1967 period, when Brown and Wilson were in close accord in dealing with the Arab–Israeli crisis. Indeed, Wilson, referring to the cabinet meeting of 23 May 1967, wrote:

> The subject was introduced by the Foreign Secretary, George Brown, at his superb best. George had never joined the majority in the Labour leadership which supported Israel, but in the Cabinet meetings during the crisis days of May and June 1967 he never wavered.[12]

George Brown was, for his part, extremely interested in Middle East affairs, on which he knew a good deal.[13] (When I was first interviewed by Brown and introduced myself as assistant under-secretary of state for Middle East affairs, he challenged me with the assertion 'I know more about the Middle East than you do,' to which I replied 'I'm delighted to hear it.' This led to the perhaps somewhat surprised Brown seeking to justify his claim, which produced an amusing conversation and eventually resulted in a good measure of mutual understanding.)

George Brown was believed by some to be of Jewish origin, although he always claimed to have Irish ancestors.[14] Whatever the truth, his wife Sophie was undoubtedly Jewish.[15] Nevertheless, although he had friends in the Israeli cabinet, made mainly at meetings of the Socialist International, which he had regularly attended, Brown's sympathies lay for the most part with the Arabs and particularly with President Nasser of Egypt, whom he had visited more than once and for whom he had a considerable admiration.[16] This made him unusual in the House of Commons, where there was a good deal of pro-Israeli feeling, especially among Labour members, together with strong anti-Nasser sentiments among many Tories, who looked back with regret on the failure of the Anglo-French invasion of the Suez Canal area in 1956.

Brown (though he does not admit it in his memoirs) came into the Foreign Office with some strange illusions about its career officials. He professed to believe that all of them had had their schooling at either Eton or Winchester. He also thought that they went out to white-tie dinner parties on most evenings and he determined to put a stop to that by keeping an unpredictable selection of them in the Office until nine o'clock whenever possible. More seriously, he held that they had twisted all foreign secretaries except Ernest Bevin around their little fingers and was determined to show that this would not happen to him. On one of his earliest days in the Foreign Office, he held a large meeting of senior officials in the old India Office Council Chamber and told them firmly 'I'm in charge.' He also then announced his determination to act without much reference to the prime minister or cabinet: 'Foreign policy will be run from this building.'[17]

One consequence of Brown's illusions was that in his early weeks in the Foreign Office he delighted in putting officials in their places, sometimes in rather unfair and unpleasant ways. This led, for instance, to the deputy under-secretary, Sir Roger Allen (a former assistant under-secretary for Middle East affairs who now dealt with Middle East matters among other subjects), soon insisting on being posted abroad, where he exchanged places with his namesake, Sir Denis Allen, ambassador to Ankara. Brown also took a particular dislike to the head of the Eastern Department of the Foreign Office in 1967, Willie Morris, an experienced and able officer whose department's responsibilities included relations with Israel and all its Arab neighbours except Egypt. I had a hard time insisting that Morris be present at meetings dealing with the Arab–Israeli problem and was finally only permitted to bring him to them on the understanding that Morris could listen but not speak. There were thus some complications in the smooth running of policy formulation in the Foreign Office, especially as Brown was a hard drinker and invariably not sober at the evening meetings that he regularly called. This was a great pity, as he was an extremely intelligent man when

at his best, and quite capable of reaching first-rate decisions about
the matters for which he was responsible. Some examples of his
good decisions will appear in subsequent chapters.

Two other ministers, both ministers of state, had responsibilities
for Middle East affairs under George Brown. In the Foreign Office
team was George Thomson, an extremely able and hard-working
minister, who had been allotted the Middle East in the partitioning
of the world between ministers of state. He was in 1968 promoted to
secretary of state for Commonwealth affairs, and was succeeded in
the Foreign Office by another hard worker, Goronwy Roberts. It
was Thomson who went first to Washington to try to persuade the
Americans to back Britain's plan for averting the June 1967 Arab–
Israeli war, as will be seen in Chapter 3.

The second of these ministers of state was Lord Caradon (Hugh
Foot, made a peer to give him a place in the parliamentary system),
who was sent to be the United Kingdom's permanent representative
to the United Nations in New York, with the personal rank of
ambassador. He, of course, dealt with the affairs of all countries of
the world which came under discussion there, but had a particular
interest in Middle East problems as he had served for eight years in
Palestine as a government official in the days of the British mandate.[18] He spoke Arabic and had personal friends in several of the
Arab delegations in New York. At the same time, he was entirely
capable of viewing Middle East affairs objectively and could get on
well with the Israeli delegation. This, as will be seen later, put him
into a strong position to deal with Arab–Israeli problems in New
York, where he rapidly built up a considerable reputation as one of
the ablest among the permanent members of the Security Council.
The combined team, Brown, Thomson and Caradon, once it had
settled down, was a strong one.

Officials in the Foreign Office

At official level, the Foreign Office in 1967 had a wise and hard-
working permanent under-secretary, Sir Paul Gore-Booth, whose
particular strengths lay in his knowledge of South Asia (he had been

United Kingdom High Commissioner in New Delhi) and in information policy. He had not served in the Middle East and made no claim to be an expert on its affairs, but he naturally took a close interest in developments there in 1967. One of his ways of keeping abreast of happenings in all areas of Foreign Office responsibility was to hold a meeting of all under-secretaries from 9.30 to 10 every morning (familiarly known to its participants as 'morning prayers').[19] This was a normal and very useful Foreign Office practice, which contributed considerably to coordination of policies between the various departments.

Below the permanent under-secretary, responsibility for Middle East policy lay particularly with one of the deputy under-secretaries, Sir Roger Allen, succeeded in 1967 by Sir Denis Allen, and with the assistant under-secretary for Middle East affairs, who at that time was myself. I supervised four Foreign Office geographical departments: the Eastern Department, which dealt with Israel, Syria, Lebanon, Jordan, Iraq and Iran; the African Department, dealing inter alia with Egypt, Sudan, Libya, Tunisia, Algeria, Morocco and Mauritania; the Arabian Department, responsible for all the countries of the Arabian Peninsula; and the Aden Department, taken over by the Foreign Office, on my proposal, from the Colonial Office in 1966, when that ministry otherwise merged with the Commonwealth Relations Office.

It is worth remarking that in 1967 the geographical departments formed the backbone of the Foreign Office. As John Coles points out:

> When I became a diplomat in 1960, the most prestigious departments in the Foreign Office were the so-called geographical departments, those that dealt with specific areas of the world such as the Middle East or the Soviet and East European countries. The great men (and they were nearly all men) were those who advised during the Arab–Israeli wars of 1967 and 1973.[20]

The only 'functional department' closely involved in the affairs dealt with in this book was the United Nations (Political) Department, whose supervising assistant under-secretary was Peter Hayman.

Something should be said about the division of work and responsibility between ministers and officials in the Foreign Office. As Wallace rightly says:

> The Foreign Secretary ... can only himself deal with the broad outline of foreign policy, selecting from the mass of Foreign Office business those few issues which his personal interest, his awareness of high-policy implications, inter-ministerial differences, or parliamentary pressures bring to the forefront of his attention.[21]

Foreign Office officials, regularly described as an 'élite', have often been thought to dominate the formulation of foreign policy along lines of their own. As Wallace says: 'Both Conservative and Labour politicians have criticised Whitehall for what they see as its imperviousness to political direction and its attachment to its own settled "views"'. Wallace goes on to say: 'Policy evolves in a continuing interaction between political direction and the pressures of established practice and administrative interests. Where political direction is clear, it is able to carry the administrative machine with it; in the absence of firm political pressures, however, administrative politics prevail.'[22] In the case of the Foreign Office under George Brown, there was never any doubt that the foreign secretary was in full charge, as he had warned his officials he would be.

It is often claimed that the Foreign Office, or at least its official level, is pro-Arab. There is an element of truth in this. What is certainly a fact is that, because there are so many Arab countries, there are a large number of senior officials in the Foreign Office who are sent to learn Arabic and have served in Arab capitals. That, as I used to point out to my Israeli contacts, does not necessarily make them pro-Arab, but it gives them some insight into Arab history and customs.[23] By contrast, few Foreign Office officials are needed to learn Hebrew and serve in the single diplomatic mission in Israel, though some of them of course, serving there or elsewhere, will be Jews. As Wallace points out:

> Half the administrative grade entrants to the Service are assigned to learn a 'hard' language, acquiring in the process a regional specialization. The largest group, and the only one with a separate training centre (the Middle East Centre for Arab Studies),[24] are the Arabists, who staff some twenty posts in North Africa and the Middle East. ... Specialists can expect to spend up to half of their careers in positions directly related to their areas, including two or three overseas postings and periods in the relevant geographical departments at home.[25]

A contributing factor was a change in personnel policy that occurred in the Foreign Service in the early 1950s. Until then few British ambassadors in Middle East posts were Arabic (or Turkish or Persian) speakers. They normally had on their staff a long-serving oriental secretary (or occasionally oriental counsellor, and, in the case of Walter Smart in Cairo, even oriental minister) who was fluent in the local language, knowledgeable about local affairs, and with a wide acquaintance of leading figures in the local population. Upon him the ambassador and senior members of his staff relied for a great deal of local guidance. However, in the early 1950s the Foreign Office decided that this was not sufficient, and that every section of a Middle East embassy should have its own fluent speaker (and reader and writer) of the local language. In due course, as promotions occurred, this would mean that senior officers in the embassies, and eventually ambassadors, would be fluent in the local languages. As a result, oriental secretaries ceased to exist as such, and the number of Arabists in the service was gradually greatly increased.

Other factors contributed to the pro-Arab tendency in the Foreign (later Diplomatic) Service. British economic interests in Arab countries far exceeded those in Israel. Oil figured largest in this respect, and there was huge British investment in Middle East oil production. Trade was also important. Britain normally had an unfavourable balance of trade with the Middle East as a whole, but the oil-rich countries there made considerable purchases from Britain (including arms) and were likely to keep at least a considerable part of their financial reserves invested in Britain.

Parliament

Parliament plays only a small role in the following chapters. There was no specialized Parliamentary Committee on Foreign Affairs in 1967–68. Debates on foreign affairs were scheduled at approximately six-monthly intervals in both the Commons and the Lords, but they tended to be wide-ranging discussions, not concentrating on a particular area of policy. Moreover, there was something of a common practice that foreign policy should to a large extent be a non-party matter. As Wallace says: 'there is a long-established parliamentary tradition that foreign policy ought to be insulated from the rough-and-tumble of domestic debate, that both government and opposition ought to seek for bi-partisan policies, that politics should stop at the water's edge.'[26] There were exceptions, such as the Suez affair in 1956, but there were no party divisions on policy in 1967. Harold Wilson records:

> In the evening [of 30 May] Edward Heath and Sir Alec Douglas-Home came to No. 10 to express their concern and to be reassured that we were doing all in our power not only to avert war, but also to stand firm on Britain's national position on the maritime rights of all nations through international waterways. From that moment the Government's policy had bipartisan backing.[27]

Embassies

Something should be said about the role of embassies. Apart from Yemen, with which diplomatic relations had been broken, there were no legations in the Middle East in 1967–68; they had all been promoted to embassies by that time. They of course act as a link with the governments to which they are accredited, passing to them information about the British government's policies. They do the same thing, in a less detailed way, for the diplomatic corps in their posts, and are greatly helped in this task by the Foreign Office practice of sending out 'Intels' (information telegrams) informing all embassies, or sometimes a geographical selection of them, about a sequence of events or a line of policy, with instructions about the use to be made of such information.

But above all, the task of embassies is to provide prompt and accurate information about the thinking and policies of the governments to which they are accredited and about press reports and popular opinion in their host countries. This regular supply of information is vital for the proper working of the geographic and other departments of the Foreign Office. As Wallace says: 'The first precondition for effective foreign policy-making is the collection of information.'[28] The work of the Foreign Office in much of 1967 was hampered by the fact that several Arab countries, including the most important of them, Egypt, had earlier broken off diplomatic relations with Britain because of its Rhodesian policy. Later many others broke off relations because of false charges of British collusion with Israel in the June 1967 war, as will be seen in Chapter 4. The rapid restoration of these relations with all Arab countries except Syria was an important achievement by George Brown in late 1967 and early 1968.

Information also reached the Foreign Office in a number of other ways. Chief among these were intelligence sources.[29] In general terms it can be said that policy makers in the government quite often had extremely valuable information about the policies and intentions of Middle Eastern governments, derived from the Special Intelligence Service (MI6) and from Government Communications Headquarters.

Authorization procedures

It is perhaps worth sounding a warning about the interpretation of Foreign Office papers released to the Public Record Office under the

30-year rule. Care must be taken if it is desired to use these papers to assess the parts played by individuals, whether ministers or officials, in the formulation and transmission of policy decisions. The papers retained in the files after their ultimate weeding, prior to their release to the Public Record Office, are normally the final versions only, without the drafts from which they are derived. This is unfortunate, since only the drafts show who actually drew up, or authorized the despatch of, the paper in question. All telegrams sent from the Foreign Office to posts abroad are signed SOSFA (Secretary of State for Foreign Affairs) and all incoming telegrams from embassies are signed with the name of the head of the mission concerned. They may, however, in reality have been authorized by somebody more junior. To know who that is, it would be necessary to see the initials at the bottom of the draft sent to the telegram section in the Foreign Office or embassy. In the case of telegrams dictated to a typist by the foreign secretary himself, these would normally be the initials of his principal private secretary.

There is a corresponding ambiguity in the case of the formal submissions sent up to the foreign secretary, or sometimes to another Foreign Office minister, by officials, to obtain a ruling on policy. These are always signed by the head of department concerned (the assistant under-secretary, the deputy under-secretary and the permanent under-secretary may make additional comments as the submission makes its way up the hierarchy). However, the paper may in fact have been drafted by one of the juniors in the relevant department, or at the other extreme the assistant under-secretary may have instructed the head of department to write it, telling him what line to follow. Unfortunately there is no way of finding this out from the final record.

Policy on Middle East affairs

Britain's reputation in the Middle East had been very badly damaged by the Suez fiasco in 1956. Thereafter, it proved possible to pick up many of the damaged political pieces over a relatively short period, but it was thought wise for Britain to keep a low profile in the Middle East for a long time to come. The United Kingdom's remaining political position in the Arab world was the target of attack by Nasser, especially in virulent broadcasts from Cairo Radio's *Sawt al-'Arab* ('Voice of the Arabs'). However, Anglo-Middle Eastern trade flourished and the major British producers of oil added to their resources in the Persian Gulf area. By 1967 the worst seemed over for Britain, by which time the government was looking forward to a period of political quiet and commercial prosperity in the region, until these hopes were shattered in May by the sudden Arab–Israeli crisis, which faced policy makers with unexpected choices. The nature of these choices and the effects on the United Kingdom of Middle Eastern developments largely outside its control are the principal subjects of this book.

CHAPTER 1

THE BACKGROUND TO BRITAIN'S SITUATION IN THE MIDDLE EAST IN 1967

IN 1967, WHAT ELIZABETH MONROE perceptively called 'Britain's Moment in the Middle East' was drawing towards an end, but had not yet quite expired.[1] Britain had granted autonomy to the emirate of Transjordan in 1923, which became fully independent as a kingdom in 1946, following its annexation of the Arab-controlled parts of Palestine. The mandate over Iraq had been ended in 1932, when Iraq joined the League of Nations under British sponsorship, although a treaty was negotiated under which Britain retained use of two air bases until 1958. An Anglo-Egyptian Treaty of 1936 had made Egypt virtually independent, although it retained special treaty rights for Britain, allowing the stationing of 10,000 troops in the British Canal Zone Base (there were in fact 80,000 there in 1954). This situation survived until 1956.

British military administration of Cyrenaica and Tripolitania in Libya was ended by the United Nations in 1951,[2] although Britain kept an air base and had overflying rights there until the 1969 revolution. The United Kingdom's mandate over Palestine (for a more detailed account of which see below) had been surrendered in 1948, when Israel declared its independence and Jordan annexed the remaining Arab areas, except the Gaza Strip which was administered but not annexed by Egypt. The Sudan, an Anglo-Egyptian condominium, had chosen independence rather than union with

Egypt in 1956. In that year too Britain completed a withdrawal of its troops from the Suez Canal Zone Base in June, and the Suez fiasco in November ended Britain's remaining hold on the civilianized base, with the British contractors expelled. In 1961 Kuwait became fully independent by terminating its treaty with Britain (although Britain in fact provided troops to defend Kuwait against an Iraqi threat shortly after its independence). In 1967 it was announced that the Federation of South Arabia, set up in 1963 by the merger of the Aden colony and the two Aden protectorates, would become independent on 9 January 1968. As George Brown's notes for a meeting of the Parliamentary Labour Party in February 1967 said, 'Aden is in a mess of Duncan Sandys' creation.[3] All we can do now is to try to keep the mess to a minimum while we get out of an intolerable situation.' Hence British political responsibility would shortly remain only in the emirates of Bahrain, Qatar and the trucial states, where Britain still controlled foreign affairs and defence.[4] There was in fact to be a small increase in forces there, for which on the same occasion George Brown had to be apologetic:

> The right way of looking at it is not that we are building up from one battalion to two in the Persian Gulf but that we are cutting down from six battalions to two in the Middle East theatre. This is a bigger cut proportionately than we are making anywhere else in the world.

Other United Kingdom interests in the Middle East were mainly economic and commercial. There were major investments in the British elements of the international oil companies operating in Iran, Kuwait, Abu Dhabi, Qatar and elsewhere in the Persian Gulf area. British oil imports from the Middle East exceeded £400 million in 1967, despite the interruptions of supply (see Chapter 4). And in the opposite direction British exports to the Middle East countries in 1966 exceeded £300 million and were running at much the same level in 1967 prior to the June war. The main importers of British goods were Israel, Iran, Kuwait and Libya. The prospects for enlarging British exports to the Middle East were very promising because of the burgeoning wealth of its oil producers. Oil and commerce were increasingly taking over from politics as the main focus of the United Kingdom's interest in the whole of the Middle East area.[5]

Britain and Palestine

Britain's involvement in Palestine had begun on 2 November 1917 with the famous (or, to the Arabs, infamous) Balfour Declaration – a letter from the British foreign secretary, Arthur Balfour, to Lord Rothschild, a leading British Zionist Jew, in which Balfour had declared that Britain viewed with favour 'the establishment in Palestine of a National Home for the Jewish people'.[6] This pledge was balanced in the same sentence by the clear statement that 'nothing shall be done which may prejudice the civil and religious rights of existing non-Jewish communities in Palestine', but this turned out to be little more than a pious aspiration: the two parts of the sentence proved irreconcilable.

Balfour himself admitted this in a memorandum of August 1919, referring to the pledges given during the war to the peoples of Syria, Palestine and Mesopotamia. These included an Anglo-French declaration of November 1918 promising 'the setting up of national governments and administrations that shall derive their authority from the free exercise of the initiative and choice of the indigenous population'. Commenting on this, Balfour said:

> The contradiction between the letter of the Covenant and the policy of the Allies is even more flagrant in the case of the independent nation of Palestine than in that of the independent nation of Syria. For in Palestine we do not propose even to go through the form of consulting the wishes of the present inhabitants of the country, though the American Commission [the American King-Crane Commission of Enquiry sent to Palestine in 1919 by President Wilson] has been going through the form of asking what they are. The four great powers are committed to Zionism and Zionism, be it right or wrong, good or bad, is rooted in age-long tradition, in present needs, in future hopes, of far profounder import

than the desires and prejudices of the 700,000 Arabs who now inhabit that ancient land. ... In fact, so far as Palestine is concerned, the powers have made no statement of fact that is not admittedly wrong, and no declaration of policy which, at least in the letter, they have not always intended to violate.[7]

Balfour's declaration of favour for a Jewish national home soon assumed an increased importance on 9 December 1917, when General Allenby entered the city of Jerusalem, signalling Turkish defeat in the Jerusalem Sanjak. Allenby entered on foot, this deliberate humility contrasting with the grand entry of the German Kaiser Wilhelm II on a white horse in 1898.[8] He was received with rapture by the local Arab population, most of whom knew nothing as yet of the Balfour Declaration, which had been largely kept secret from them. They played with his name, converting it into 'Allah' and 'nabi' (prophet).[9] Their eyes were soon opened by the arrival in Palestine in March 1918 of the Zionist Commission, under Chaim Weizmann, sent to arrange for the establishment of the Jewish national home.[10] Ronald Storrs, then governor of Jerusalem under the Occupied Enemy Territory Administration, arranged for the commission to meet Arab dignitaries, including the mayor of Jerusalem and the *mufti.*[11]

By the end of October 1918 the Allies had driven the Turkish Seventh Army out of the whole of Syria, and the Levant provinces of the Ottoman Empire lay open to partition between the victors.[12] That partition had in fact been preordained in 1916 by the Sykes–Picot Agreement, which secretly allotted the provinces in question to division between Britain and France. France was to get Syria and Lebanon and Britain's share was Iraq and Transjordan, later revised to include Palestine following the British conquest of that area.[13] This division was legalized after the war by mandates from the League of Nations.

The promise of a national home for the Jews was written into the League of Nations mandate for Palestine, which Britain obtained on 5 May 1920. Inevitably its inclusion infuriated the indigenous Arab population of the country, which witnessed with growing alarm Jewish migration to Palestine. The Jewish minority in Palestine had fallen during the war from some 80,000 in 1914 to around 65,000 at the time of the Balfour Declaration in 1917. The national home depended from the beginning on an assumption of large-scale Jewish immigration to swell these numbers.[14] It began relatively slowly, with only 1,806 in 1919, and between 8,000 and 8,500 a year in the next four years.[15]

Although the mandate system presumed that the mandated territories would be brought to independence, Britain administered Palestine after the fashion of a crown colony. The Colonial Office was the responsible ministry in Whitehall and all senior posts in the Palestine Service were manned by Britons, many of them ex-army officers. British judges presided in the upper courts and British officers commanded the police. The only non-colonial feature of the administration was that the king's representative was called a high commissioner instead of a governor.[16] It was perhaps tactless of the British government to appoint a Jew, Sir Herbert Samuel, as the first high commissioner, although in practice he tended to demonstrate his impartiality by favouring the Arab side in any Arab–Jewish dispute.[17] One important decision, which he took in March 1921, was to back the election as *mufti* of Jerusalem of Muhammad Amin Al-Hussaini, usually known as Haj Amin, a young man who had earlier been condemned *in absentia* to 15 years' imprisonment for inciting Arab Palestinians to anti-Zionist violence.[18] This naturally aroused bitter Jewish criticism.

The Hussaini family, which claimed descent from Caliph Ali and his wife Fatima, daughter of the prophet Muhammad, was one of the two leading families of Jerusalem, the other being the Nashashibis, whose leading figure, Raghib al-Nashashibi, was then mayor of Jerusalem. Partly to keep the balance between the two families, some of Samuel's advisers urged him to appoint Haj Amin as *mufti*, in principle a purely religious appointment. But Haj Amin was an ambitious man. He not only demanded, and was granted, the title of

Grand Mufti, a British invention which had earlier been held by his brother, but succeeded in being appointed additionally president of the Supreme Muslim Council, giving him extensive patronage over appointments of religious officials and control of the *waqf* (charity) system. In that capacity, he won great acclaim by raising funds for the restoration of the two mosques of the Haram al Sharif (the noble sanctuary), which stood on the former site of Herod's temple.[19]

In January 1921 Emir Abdullah Ibn Hussein, of the ruling family in the Hejaz, formed an army of 2,000 men at Ma'an, just within the Hejaz border close to Transjordan, and announced that he would march across Transjordan to Damascus to avenge the insult to his family of the expulsion by the French of his younger brother Feisal from the throne of Syria. He did not succeed in this project, nor even seriously attempt it, but in Transjordan he managed to unite the petty principalities then existing there and was acclaimed prince of these territories.[20] In March 1921, at a conference held in Cairo, this situation was accepted by the British colonial secretary, Winston Churchill. At the same time, the expelled Feisal was appointed king of Iraq, subject to the outcome of an Iraqi referendum which welcomed him. Churchill went from Cairo to Palestine and met Emir Abdullah in Jerusalem. Abdullah agreed to acknowledge the British mandate in Transjordan, to accept financial aid and a small degree of British guidance, and to abandon his plan to attack the French in Damascus.[21] This had the effect of splitting Transjordan administratively from Palestine, to the disappointment of the more extreme Zionists who had hoped to establish a Jewish state in the whole mandate area, but at the time this was an extremely distant objective. In September 1922 the Council of the League of Nations confirmed these arrangements by accepting a United Kingdom proposal that Transjordan should be exempted from the mandate clauses regarding the establishment of a Jewish national home in Palestine.[22]

By the spring of 1925 the Jewish population of Palestine, which had been some 55,000 in 1918, had risen to 108,000.[23] A Jewish

Agency had been formed to administer what in practice soon amounted to a state within a state. The Jewish community levied its own taxes, set up its own schools, raised its own military unit, the *Haganah* (defence), and operated a highly efficient intelligence service, which thoroughly penetrated the British administration. One of the great Jewish successes was to re-establish Hebrew as the language of the community, thus differentiating it from the Arabs and contributing to internal autonomy, since it was a language unknown to virtually all the British officials.[24] In 1925 a Hebrew university was formally opened in Jerusalem. The attendance of Lord Balfour at the opening ceremony caused the Arabs to mount a general strike in protest.[25]

Serious Arab rioting against the Jews occurred in 1928, touched off by a dispute at the Wailing Wall, the only surviving remnant of Herod's temple, holy to the Jews and sensitive to the Arabs since it marked the boundary of their own holy area, the Haram al Sharif, the site of the Dome of the Rock (from which the prophet Muhammad was reputed to have ascended on a flying visit to heaven) and of the Al-Aqsa Mosque. Neither the police nor the *Haganah* could restrain the violence, which was particularly brutal in Hebron and Safad, where there were long-standing (and largely anti-Zionist) religious Jewish communities. Six Jewish *kibbutzim* (agricultural settlements) were wiped out. In all, 133 Jews were killed and 339 wounded. British troops were hastily transferred from Egypt to suppress the disorders, and the Arabs for their part suffered 116 killed and 232 wounded. Twenty-seven Arab perpetrators were convicted and sentenced to death, but only three of the death sentences were carried out.[26]

The British government sent out a commission of inquiry, under Sir Walter Shaw, to look into these unhappy events. The commission ascribed the outbreak to widespread Arab hostility towards the Jews, with the Arabs fearing that continuing Jewish immigration and land purchases would ultimately transform the Arab population into a landless minority. The colonial secretary, Lord Passfield, in October 1930 issued a white paper imposing stricter controls on immigration and land transfers and declaring that future immigration would depend upon 'economic absorptive capacity'.[27] This naturally roused a storm of Jewish protest, to which the British government succumbed, issuing in February 1931 a 'clarification' of the white paper which largely cancelled out its pro-Arab provisions.[28]

The rise to power of Adolf Hitler as Chancellor of Germany at the end of January 1933 complicated the British task in Palestine immensely. His initial policy against German Jews was to deprive them of their property and jobs and put pressure on them to leave the Reich. Immigration into Palestine in 1933 more than tripled, to no less than 30,327. In August 1933 the Zionist Conference, meeting in Prague, passed resolutions demanding the urgent building of the Jewish national home on a far larger scale than before. The Arab Executive in Palestine (set up as a counter to the Jewish Agency) organized a general strike, and riots occurred in several areas of Palestine, forcibly suppressed by the police.[29]

In April 1936 a serious Arab revolt against the British administration broke out in Palestine. It was a campaign largely of sabotage and spasmodic attacks, often by snipers. Roads were mined, trains were blown up, crops and trees were burnt, telephone and telegraph lines were cut. Government informers were almost entirely silenced by threats and assassinations. As in 1928, troop reinforcements were rushed in, raising the Palestine garrison to some 20,000 men. Emergency regulations authorized searches without warrant, collective punishments and severe penalties for possessing weapons.[30] With the use of such measures, the violence was held in check and it finally petered out with the outbreak of the Second World War in September 1939.[31]

One effect of the Arab Revolt had been to strip away Haj Amin's claim to be a restraining influence on Arab violence. He was compelled to declare himself as the Revolt's leader and was in imminent danger of arrest. To escape it, he made his way to Jaffa in disguise and got away from there to Lebanon.[32] (From there, when the

Second World War broke out, he escaped, again in disguise, to Iraq, where he was involved in the Rashid Ali coup, suppressed by the British army. He took refuge in Iran and was flown by the Germans from there to Germany.[33])

The 1936 Arab Revolt had produced a major rethink about Palestine by the British government. The Peel Commission in 1937 for the first time recommended a partition of Palestine into Jewish and Arab states, to the horror of the Arabs and not entirely to the pleasure of the Jews. This recommendation was approved by the cabinet on 7 July 1937, on the advice of the Colonial Office under its secretary of state, William Ormsby-Gore.[34] But cabinet approval on this occasion did not prove decisive, since it masked the antagonism to the proposal of the Foreign Office under its more powerful secretary of state, Anthony Eden.[35] The Eastern Department of the Foreign Office was responsible for the foreign relations of Palestine and had been headed since 1930 by an experienced bureaucrat, George W. Rendel. He was mindful of the views of the Arab countries, which were opposed to partition of what they regarded as Arab Palestine, and (most improperly) he set himself to oppose implementation of the cabinet decision.

In-fighting between the Foreign and Colonial Offices did in fact delay implementation until at a cabinet meeting on 7 December 1937 a compromise was reached whereby a technical commission was to be appointed and sent to Palestine to look into the details of the partition plan. The Foreign Office was clear that this technical commission, with well-chosen members, would be likely to report that partition was impractical.[36] In effect, the Peel Commission's recommendations were shelved. They were finally abandoned when a League of Nations Commission declared them unworkable and the British government agreed that this was so.

After the failure of conferences on Palestine in London with the Jews and Arabs (the presence at which of representatives of Arab states was a constitutional innovation), the government issued a white paper in May 1939, which provided for the limitation of

Jewish immigration into Palestine to 75,000 over the next five years, after which further immigration would be subject to Arab 'acquiescence'. This was rejected by the Arabs and even more strongly by the Jews, who regarded it as a betrayal of the Balfour Declaration.[37]

During the Second World War, some 27,000 Palestinian Jews enlisted in the British forces and a Jewish munitions industry was set up to supply arms to Britain's Middle East Command, thus reducing the need for British shipping. However, Britain long rejected the request for the formation of a Jewish army, flying the Zionist flag.[38] Only in 1944 was permission given for the formation of a Jewish brigade of the British army, which fought under the command of the Eighth Army in Italy.[39]

Illegal Jewish immigrants into Palestine were deported by the British authorities, and this led to terrorist attacks on the latter by the semi-secret Jewish *Haganah* and the even more extreme Stern Gang. Their exploits included the assassination in Cairo in November 1944 of the British minister resident in the Middle East, Lord Moyne.[40]

Another crucial development during the Second World War was the transfer of the headquarters of the international Zionist Movement from Britain to the United States. This was the decision of David Ben Gurion, who had emerged as the leader of the new generation of Zionists. A Zionist conference held in New York in May 1944 adopted a programme calling for unrestricted immigration and the establishment of Palestine as a Jewish commonwealth.[41] Ben Gurion was looking for United States pressure on Britain to achieve his postwar aspirations for the creation of a Jewish state in Palestine.

After the Second World War, the world became aware of the horrors of the Holocaust. This naturally increased pressure for the survivors of European Jewry to be admitted to Palestine, and the United States Congress urged unlimited access. President Truman wrote to Prime Minister Attlee recommending the issuing of 100,000 certificates of immigration to Palestine.[42] The British government, on the initiative of Foreign Secretary Ernest Bevin, who would have preferred to see the Jewish refugees resettled in Europe and the United States, countered by proposing the creation of a joint commission to study the problem, including the absorptive capacity of Palestine. The appointment of this commission was announced by Bevin to the House of Commons on 13 November 1945.[43] It worked from January to April 1946, with Richard Crossman as one of its British members. On 30 April it issued a unanimous report recommending the immediate entry into Palestine of 100,000 Jewish immigrants, the conversion of the British mandate into a United Nations trusteeship territory and the maintenance of Palestine as, in effect, a bi-national state with equal Jewish and Arab representation. Truman at once announced that he accepted the 100,000 immigrants recommendation, but made no mention of the other features of the report. Attlee, who was furious that this American announcement had been made without consultation with Britain, stated the next day in the Commons that the British government would not proceed to implement the report until private armies in Palestine were disbanded.[44]

Attlee's statement reflected his anxieties about the internal security situation in Palestine. When Britain had continued to resist illegal immigration, the Jewish underground forces had resumed their activities, culminating in the *Irgun Zvai Leumi* blowing up the King David Hotel in Jerusalem, a wing of which housed the Palestine administration, on 22 July 1946. In this incident, 91 people were killed, among them 21 senior government officials, and 46 injured.[45] It was probably this catastrophe more than anything else that undermined the British government's will to continue the Palestine mandate, although it survived for another 18 months. Jewish terrorism continued, and, for security reasons, British officials' wives and children were evacuated from Palestine in March 1947.[46]

Ben Gurion had been pleased with the Anglo-American commission's recommendation on the 100,000 immigrant certificates and with Truman's endorsement of it, but dissatisfied with its failure to recommend what he considered even more important: a Jewish state.[47] Zionist pressure in the United States was exercised in the direction of partition and Truman's thoughts began to move in that direction. On 4 October 1946, on the eve of the Jewish festival of *Yom Kippur* (the day of atonement) and Congressional elections, he issued a statement in which he supported 'the creation of a viable Jewish state in control of its own immigration and economic policies in an adequate area of Palestine instead of the whole of Palestine'. The State Department had managed to insert into the statement the idea that the United States hoped to see a bridging of the gap between the British and the Zionist proposals, but this attracted no attention in the American press.[48] Bevin did not react to the statement, as his own mind was now turning to use of the United Nations machinery, and he did not believe that there could be a two-thirds majority in the General Assembly for the creation of a Jewish state in Palestine.[49]

In February 1947 Britain referred the problem to the United Nations, as successor to the League of Nations which had granted Britain the original mandate over Palestine.[50] A United Nations Special Commission on Palestine was set up which, contrary to British expectations, reported on 1 September recommending the partition of Palestine into Arab and Jewish states, with Jerusalem and its environs excluded from both as a *corpus separatum*. The Jewish community was to have Eastern Galilee, the coastal strip and the Negev Desert, while the Arabs were to have Upper and Western Galilee, the West Bank and the Gaza Strip.[51] This plan, with minor changes, was adopted on 29 November 1947 as United Nations General Assembly Resolution 181, by 33 votes to 13 with 10 abstentions.[52]

On 26 September 1947 the British colonial secretary, Creech Jones, had announced to the United Nations that the British government would terminate the mandate. Following the UN vote of 29 November, they fixed the date for this as 15 May 1948 and in fact completed evacuation on 14 May. They had meanwhile to witness communal fighting in Palestine in which the better organized and more ruthless Jews were the more successful, capturing Tiberias, Haifa, Acre, Jaffa and the modern part of Jerusalem.[53] Among other events in this civil war was the capture by the Jews of the Arab village of Deir Yassin on 9 April 1948, with the entire population shot or expelled.[54] The news of this calculated atrocity caused terror throughout the Arab population of Palestine and, as was no doubt intended, led to a major exodus of Arab refugees.[55]

As soon as the mandate formally ended, the Jews proclaimed the State of Israel, which was quickly recognized by the United States and the Soviet Union. Units of the Egyptian, Syrian, Transjordanian and Iraqi regular armies crossed the frontiers in an attempt to save the situation. Their objective was to restore order and at least to protect the 45 per cent of Palestine allotted to the Arabs in the United Nations partition plan. After some initial successes they were outfought and by January 1949 only 21 per cent of Palestine remained in Arab hands.[56]

A United Nations mediator, the American Ralph Bunche, succeeded between February and July 1949 in negotiating armistice agreements between Israel and its Arab neighbours (Iraq made no agreement but withdrew its troops from Palestine). Transjordan, at the invitation of some 2,000 Palestinian notables in Jericho, annexed the remaining Arab territories on the West Bank of the River Jordan, changing the country's name to the Kingdom of Jordan. The Gaza Strip was held but not annexed by the Egyptians. About half of the Arab population of Palestine had fled the country to Jordan, Lebanon, Syria and the Gaza Strip as refugees. After the United Nations had failed to negotiate a peace treaty under their auspices, Israel was admitted to membership of the organization on 11 May 1949.[57]

The *nakba* (catastrophe), as the Arabs called it, was largely blamed on Britain. As they saw it, the British government had issued the Balfour Declaration, had accepted the Palestine mandate, had (if in part reluctantly) acquiesced in the immigration of tens of thousands of Jews, had suppressed the Arab Revolt of 1936–39 and had finally surrendered the mandate with no proper provision for what was to follow it. Some blame was also attached to the United States, but overwhelmingly Britain was regarded by the Arabs as the chief culprit.[58]

Britain's collusion with Israel in the 1956 Suez affair (the aftermath of which is dealt with in Chapter 2) naturally reinforced these anti-British sentiments. British ministers' attempts to deny the collusion, which were believed nowhere in the Arab world, gave Britain additionally a reputation as a persistent liar. It must be remembered that all these attitudes were still fresh in Arab minds in 1967 (see particularly Chapter 4). They made it easier for Arabs then to believe what were in fact false charges of a new British collusion with Israel, with British denials regarded merely as renewed lying.

CHAPTER 2

NASSER'S
MISCALCULATIONS

PRESIDENT GAMAL ABDEL NASSER OF EGYPT prided himself on being a realist. He had warned Syria and Jordan that the Egyptian army, which he had re-armed with Soviet weaponry by 1967, would not be ready for war with Israel for well over a year. Moreover, about a third of it, and the best third at that, had been sent to the Yemen to fight for the republican side in the civil war against the royalist forces backed by Saudi Arabia.

At the same time, he prided himself on being the supreme leader of the Arabs. It was true that the United Arab Republic of Egypt and Syria had broken down, with Syria resuming its independence, but the UAR title was still retained by Egypt for all official purposes. Nasser controlled in Cairo the most influential media resources in the region and called his main radio transmission *Sawt al-'Arab* ('Voice of the Arabs'). It was listened to all over the Arab world.

Nasser thus faced a dilemma in deciding how to react to Israeli reprisals against guerrilla attacks launched on Israel from Syria and Jordan. Both those countries looked to him for help, but he did not wish to be engaged yet in a war with Israel. Moreover, there was no obvious way in which he could even threaten Israel, since the Egyptian–Israeli border was occupied by the United Nations Emergency Force (UNEF), which had been created in 1956 to supervise Israeli withdrawal from Sinai after the conquest of that peninsula during the Suez campaign. Jordanian Radio struck a sensitive spot in Nas-

15

ser's psychology when it accused him of 'hiding behind the skirts of UNEF'.

Syria, under a Baathist regime since February 1966, had been encouraging Palestinian *fida'iyin* (commandos) to mount guerrilla raids on Israel, both from Syrian territory and from Jordan (against the will of Jordan's King Hussein). Israeli policy was to meet these raids with infrequent but severe reprisals against the states from which they had been mounted. One such attack against Syria took place in September 1966. Nasser, under criticism from Syria for failing to deter Israel, entered into an Egyptian–Syrian defence agreement on 4 December 1966. Politically that strengthened his standing in the Arab world, but, given Nasser's knowledge of the unreadiness of his armed forces, it was undoubtedly a miscalculation. It gave Egypt a commitment to help defend Syria with no corresponding control over Syrian policy.

Shortly after this agreement was signed, Israel struck against Samu' in Jordan on 13 November in response to Palestinian guerrilla raids from Jordanian territory. The attack was mishandled and there was serious fighting with the Jordanian army. The Israelis were drawn into a heavier engagement than they had intended. In the course of it, they killed 14 Jordanian soldiers and six civilians, and destroyed 41 buildings.

There was some shame for this in Israel, especially as the Israelis knew that it was Syria rather than Jordan that was responsible for the guerrilla action. Israel decided that their next reprisal must be against Syria and this occurred on 7 April 1967, when it launched an air attack, shooting down six Syrian MiG aircraft, two of them within sight of Damascus. Israeli politicians followed this up with public warnings to Syria, two of them from the prime minister and defence minister, Levi Eshkol. Arab opinion was particularly incensed by a reported warning from Yitzhak Rabin, the Israeli chief of staff, that 'We will carry out a lightning attack on Syria, occupy Damascus, overthrow the regime there and come back.' Rabin denied using this particular wording, but the report was universally believed in Arab circles and raised tension enormously. Despite the Egyptian–Syrian defence agreement of the previous November, Egypt took no action in the face of this air raid on Syria and Israel's inflammatory warnings, except for anti-Israeli diatribes on Cairo Radio. But Nasser was seriously disturbed by the loss of face that resulted from his inaction.

Against this background, a strange development occurred in May 1967. On about 8 May Syrian intelligence officers informed their Egyptian counterparts that Israel was planning an attack on Syria. Nasser ordered his own intelligence to investigate. On 13 May the Soviet Union passed to Egypt detailed reports that Israel had massed 11–13 brigades of troops in Galilee for an invasion of Syria. These reports, which were totally untrue, were communicated at a high level, both in Cairo and in Moscow. Nasser should not have been misled by them, since such a large mobilization would have visibly disrupted daily life in Israel, and of this, as his own intelligence reported, there was no sign. He was told by the Americans and others that the reports were false, but surprisingly he continued to believe them.[1]

In this belief Nasser made what turned out to be a serious miscalculation. He ordered two divisions of his army to move into Sinai to join the one division already there. His purpose was to deter the Israelis from attacking Syria by threatening them with a war on two fronts. However, this threat was scarcely credible so long as Egyptian forces in Sinai were separated from the Israeli border by UNEF. Nasser decided to remove this barrier. On 16 May 1967 a letter was delivered from the Egyptian chief of staff, General Mohammed Fawzi, to UNEF's Indian commander, General Indar Jit Rikhye, calling on him to withdraw his men from the observation posts on the Egyptian–Israeli border. The letter made no mention of UNEF's posts elsewhere, in the Gaza Strip and particularly at Sharm al-Shaikh, where UNEF controlled the entrance to the Gulf of Aqaba and kept it open to all, including Israeli shipping.[2]

Rikhye rightly replied that he could only remove his men from their observation posts on instructions from the United Nations. He reported the letter he had received to the secretary-general, U Thant. It was now U Thant's turn to make a miscalculation. In the hope, presumably, of persuading Nasser to think again, he sent for the Egyptian delegate to the United Nations, Ambassador Mohamed Awad El-Kony, and warned him that if he received from the United Arab Republic government a request on the lines of the letter to Rikhye, he would have to withdraw UNEF entirely, from the Gaza Strip and Sharm al-Shaikh as well.

This attempt to call Nasser's bluff through his ambassador was a complete failure. U Thant would have done better to have flown immediately to Cairo, to speak to Nasser direct. As he should have realized, Nasser could not change course without an intolerable loss of face in the Arab world. Inevitably the outcome was a formal request on 18 May 1967, signed by the Egyptian foreign minister, Mahmoud Riad, for the total withdrawal of UNEF. U Thant consulted his UNEF Advisory Council, consisting of the ambassadors of the countries contributing troops to UNEF, but did not summon the General Assembly or the Security Council. The Advisory Council was divided, but it too did not refer the issue to the General Assembly. With no further ado, U Thant on 18 May ordered UNEF to cease operations and prepare to leave Egypt.[3]

The secretary-general's decision was much deplored by many, including the British prime minister, Harold Wilson.[4] But U Thant based himself on the legal point that a United Nations force could not operate on a country's soil without that country's consent. This was certainly the basis on which U Thant's predecessor, Dag Hammarskjöld, had established UNEF in 1956, although he had warned the Egyptian foreign minister of the day, Mahmoud Fawzi, that the Security Council would have a role to play if Egypt requested withdrawal.[5] (Israel had refused to have UNEF on its territory, so Egypt alone was the host nation.)

Nasser was almost certainly among those surprised by U Thant's precipitate action. It seems clear that he was not really seeking a war with Israel. The Egyptian forces in Sinai were ordered to do no more than take up defensive positions until and unless Israel invaded Syria. He told Anthony Nutting, who interviewed him at this stage, that he was convinced that all would calm down provided that he did not provoke Israel further.[6] He probably expected the Security Council to be convened and to put pressure on Egypt and Israel, to which he could have yielded without loss of face. On that too he miscalculated.

Nasser was now faced with another dilemma. With UNEF withdrawing from Sharm al-Shaikh, he had no alternative but to send Egyptian troops there. And having thus re-occupied it, he was bound to declare the Gulf of Aqaba closed to Israeli shipping and to shipping bound for the Israeli port of Elath. This he knew to be a highly dangerous course of action. The Israelis had declared many times that (with the Suez Canal closed to them) Elath was their outlet to Africa and Asia and that they would not tolerate any interference with the free passage of shipping to and from it. The Egyptian blockade of the Gulf of Aqaba was therefore likely to be a *casus belli*. Nasser's action was of course hailed as a triumph throughout the Arab world and he basked in the hero-worship it brought him. But he had reason to be a worried man. Surprisingly, considering his earlier views, he seems to have let himself be reassured by the confidence of his minister of defence, Abdel Hakim Amer, that the Egyptian forces could withstand any Israeli attack.[7] If so, this was another, and fatal, miscalculation.

CHAPTER 3

BRITAIN'S ATTEMPT
TO AVERT WAR

FROM AS EARLY AS 18 MAY 1967, when U Thant ordered UNEF to cease operating, the British Foreign Office, under George Brown, had realized that its withdrawal from Sharm al-Shaikh would lead to an Egyptian closure of the Gulf of Aqaba and that that for Israel would be a *casus belli.* Brown quickly determined that Britain must do all it could to prevent an outbreak of war.[1] This was its duty as a permanent member of the Security Council. It was also directly in Britain's interest, since war would be damaging to the United Kingdom both politically and economically – politically because the Arabs still held it responsible for the creation of Israel (and Brown, rightly as it proved, expected Israel to win such a war), and economically because Britain's oil supplies came predominantly from the Middle East through the Suez Canal, which was likely to be blocked if war broke out.

There was also a still greater threat: the United States might become involved to safeguard its Israeli friends, and the Soviet Union to protect its Arab clients. Against the background of the tension between these two superpowers, already heightened by Vietnam, an Arab–Israeli war could escalate into a global conflict.

Brown decided that the right course was for the United Kingdom to take the lead at once in organizing an international consortium of the major maritime nations, which would bring pressure on Egypt to allow trade to continue to pass unhindered through the Straits of Tiran at the mouth of the Gulf of Aqaba.[2] This would be consistent

with the declarations of the main maritime powers in the United
Nations in 1957, including that of the United Kingdom's permanent
representative to the United Nations. He also concluded that such
pressure was unlikely to be effective unless Egypt was convinced
that in the last resort the consortium would use force to secure
transit through the Gulf of Aqaba to Elath.[3]

This conclusion was notable because Brown had the reputation
of being pro-Arab and particularly pro-Nasser, whereas intervening
to keep open the Gulf of Aqaba would be seen throughout the Arab
world as pro-Israeli and anti-Nasser.[4] It also overrode Brown's
estimate of the likely hostile reactions of the Arab oil-producer states
from which Britain drew the bulk of its oil supplies, including those
Persian Gulf emirates for whose foreign affairs Britain was still
responsible. It was thus a major departure from Britain's general
policy at the time, which was to keep a low profile on the Arab–
Israeli conflict. In Brown's view, the crisis had, at least for the
present, outdated that policy and the time had come for decisive
action.

On enquiry, Brown found Harold Wilson, who had the reputation of being somewhat pro-Israeli, sympathetic to this line of
thought.[5] Richard Crossman, the Lord President of the Council,
was, as he was the first to admit, entirely pro-Israeli in his approach
to Middle East affairs.[6] He had become a non-Jewish Zionist while
serving as one of the six British members of the Anglo-American
Committee of Inquiry into Palestine in 1945–46. As he wrote to Mrs
Myerson (Golda Meir) on 24 June 1946, 'It looks as though Palestine
for me was not merely a matter of 120 days, but has become a life-
long obligation.'[7] In his diaries, published in 1976, he claimed that
the cabinet minutes of these 1967 meetings were 'misleading', by
which he seems to have meant incomplete.[8] To our great benefit, he
set out to be more enlightening than the cabinet papers on how the
discussions had gone.[9]

He made it clear that Wilson and Brown wished to move British
naval units immediately to threatening positions, but that the secre-

tary of state for defence, Denis Healey, after consulting his chiefs of
staff, advised that Britain just did not have the forces to do this on its
own.[10] It would, moreover, clearly have been a more than delicate
matter, as was pointed out in the cabinet discussion, to have deployed an aircraft carrier and its supporting ships through the
Egyptian Suez Canal to outface Egypt itself.[11] Any British escort
force would therefore have had to have consisted of less powerful
vessels, which happened to be already available east of the Canal
(mainly deployed for the blockade of oil supplies to Beira during the
crisis caused by Rhodesia's unilateral declaration of independence).

The Foreign Office then prepared a revised proposal for cabinet,
recommending efforts to obtain a new declaration of the major
maritime powers in the United Nations, similar to the statements
made there in 1957 regarding freedom of navigation in the Gulf of
Aqaba, combined with contingency plans for the use of Anglo-
American naval forces.[12] The Ministry of Defence set to work on the
contingency planning, with the chiefs of staff approving a quite
detailed paper on the subject on 29 May.[13] It was clear from it that
an escort force would face considerable hazards, and that there were
real dangers of escalation. (A fairly full copy of this paper is contained in Appendix A.)

The cabinet on 30 May, led by Healey and (as he claims) Crossman, further watered down the revised Foreign Office proposal. The
prime minister happened to be already due to visit Ottawa for the
centenary of the Canadian Confederation and had arranged to go on
from there to Washington DC. He was authorized by the cabinet
merely to seek support for a declaration by the maritime powers and
to do no more than contingency probing of Canadian and US opinions about the use of force. He was to make it clear that Britain was
looking for widespread maritime support and would not participate
in a purely Anglo-American naval force to open the Gulf.[14] (Nor, as
it turned out, would the Americans.[15])

The foreign secretary had already flown to Moscow on 23 May,
on a pre-arranged official visit, before the final cabinet meeting just

described. Brown had reminded Aleksei Kosygin, the chairman of the Soviet Council of Ministers, on 24 May, that Israel had frequently declared that closure of the Gulf of Aqaba would be a *casus belli*, and he had urged the Soviet government to press Nasser not to declare a boycott in the Gulf of Aqaba. The Soviet team looked embarrassed but gave no commitment.[16] It was strange that they did not react more understandingly to Brown's plea, given their own requirement for transit through the Dardanelles. But they seem to have underestimated the importance to Israel of the Gulf of Aqaba. Alexei Vassiliev, with good access to Soviet policy makers, says:

> As far as Soviet strategic interests were concerned it made no difference who controlled the Straits of Tiran and whether or not Israeli ships could sail there. The USSR was therefore ready to support any compromise solution, considering that it was not permissible to start a war simply because a few ships were unable to sail from Aqaba to the Red Sea.[17]

However that may be, on 25 May Kosygin, without specific mention of the Gulf of Aqaba, did in fact warn the Egyptians in general terms not to commit aggression,[18] and this seems to have been decisive in making Nasser plan (unwisely from a military point of view) to leave it to Israel to strike the first blow.[19] By that time he had some 80,000 or more troops in Sinai, which he evidently thought capable of withstanding an Israeli preemptive strike.

There is also a report from Salah Bassiouny, then working in the Egyptian Foreign Ministry, that when he visited Moscow as a member of an Egyptian delegation from 24 to 28 May, the Soviet officials not only urged them to de-escalate the crisis but specifically recommended that they 'open the strait [of Tiran] for oil shipments to Israel'.[20]

George Thomson, minister of state at the Foreign Office, accompanied by Rear-Admiral Bartosik of the Royal Navy, had flown to Washington on 24 May for preliminary talks with Eugene Rostow, the United States under-secretary of state for political affairs.

Thomson, who was joined in Washington by Admiral Sir Nigel Henderson, outlined British thinking about a possible multinational naval force to escort shipping through the Straits of Tiran.[21] This idea did not appeal to the Pentagon representative present (preoccupied with Vietnam), but Rostow, who soon nicknamed the proposed force 'the Red Sea Regatta', was enthusiastic about it.[22] He later wrote:

> The idea of an Allied naval escort plan to carry out the guarantees of 1957 was first broached by George Brown, the British Foreign Minister at the time, a man of vision whose foibles and eccentricities, extraordinary as they are, are more than outweighed by his good sense and courage. Brown's idea received strong support in many parts of the American government. Both Johnson and Rusk were vigorous advocates.[23]

President Johnson himself also mentioned Thomson's visit in his memoirs. He said:

> The British proposed two steps. First, there would be a public declaration, signed by as many nations as possible, reasserting the right of free passage through the Gulf of Aqaba. There was hope that the declaration might be endorsed by the United Nations. Second, a naval task force would be set up, composed of as many nations as possible, to break Nasser's blockade and open the Strait of Tiran. During the next few days we explored the British proposal fully with key Congressmen and other interested Governments.[24]

Johnson advocated the British idea to Prime Minister Lester Pearson of Canada, whom he visited on 25 May, but found no enthusiasm for it in Ottawa.[25]

On 24 May the Israeli foreign minister, Abba Eban, set out for Washington, via Paris, to explore the possibility of solving the Straits of Tiran problem through diplomatic rather than military means.[26] He arrived at Orly Airport at 7 a.m. local time and saw the French president, Charles de Gaulle, later that morning. France had become a major supplier of arms to Israel, particularly Mystère aircraft, but the Israelis had been disappointed by France's lack of reaction to the withdrawal of UNEF and the imposition of the blockade of Elath.[27] Even before they were introduced to each other, de Gaulle said loudly to Eban 'Ne faites pas la guerre' ('Do not make war'). He went on, after an exchange of greetings, to declare that it would be catastrophic for Israel to attack, and that the dispute must be resolved by the four powers, of whom he had already proposed a meeting (rejected shortly afterwards by Moscow).

Eban explained the Israeli position, emphasizing that Israel would not be opening hostilities if it attacked, since, in their view, these had already been opened by Egypt's declaration of the blockade of Elath. De Gaulle replied that by opening hostilities he meant firing the first shot. As for the blockade, he agreed that France's 1957 declaration on freedom of navigation in the Gulf of Aqaba was juridically correct, but '1967 was not 1957'. Israel should give France time to act through consultation between the four powers, since the Soviet Union must be brought to cooperate in concerted action to enable ships to transit the Straits of Tiran.[28]

The British government had heard news of Eban's journey and had invited him to pass through London. He was promised immediate access to the prime minister and knew that opinion in Britain was overwhelmingly favourable to Israel in the present crisis. With the disappointment of France still rancouring, he decided to balance his experiences by going to see Harold Wilson.[29]

When they met, Eban found the atmosphere in Downing Street in sharp contrast to that at the Elysée Palace. Wilson told him that a cabinet meeting that morning had decided that Britain would join with others in an effort to open the Straits of Tiran. He had already sent George Thomson to Washington to explore the possibilities of common action with the Americans. Wilson did not offer Israel any advice on whether to use force (a reticence of which Eban approved), but Eban assured him that if Israel had to fight it would win. Reporting on this conversation to his government through the Israeli ambassador in London, Eban warned his government colleagues that although the chances of international support had been strengthened by this encouraging British attitude, the effectiveness of such support would depend on the American reaction.[30]

When he reached Kennedy Airport in New York the next day, Eban assured journalists that 'Israel would not expect American soldiers to lose their lives on Israel's behalf'.[31] He knew that this was a statement that would be welcomed by the United States administration. He then flew on to Washington.

There, Eban found that President Johnson was absent on an official visit to Canada but would be returning that day. To his surprise, he received a telegram from Jerusalem describing the military situation on the frontier in alarming terms. He was asked so to inform the United States government and to enquire whether an attack on Israel would be considered as an attack on the United States. He was amazed that the military situation could have so deteriorated in 48 hours and knew that President Johnson had no constitutional power to promise what Jerusalem sought.[32] A second telegram in even more emphatic terms reinforced his instructions.[33] He asked for an early meeting with Secretary of State Dean Rusk and spoke as directed. Rusk was equally surprised. He reported that the Senate Foreign Relations Committee had that morning favoured supporting Israel, but only on condition that the United States would not be acting alone. He would of course inform the president of what Eban had said.[34]

The next morning, Eban met Secretary of Defense Robert McNamara at the Pentagon, who said that the American assessment was that the Egyptian forces in Sinai were not yet deployed for an early assault. He believed that the Egyptians were waiting to see what Israel would do and that time was on Israel's side, with no urgency for a 'now or never' decision.[35]

Eban finally saw President Johnson on the evening of 26 May. He knew that he was talking to a friend of Israel.[36] That had been Johnson's reputation from his days in the Senate.[37] As president, he had appointed American Jews to many important posts in his ad-

ministration, such as the Rostow brothers – Walt, his national
security adviser, and Eugene, under-secretary of state for political
affairs in the State Department. Another Jew was Ambassador
Arthur Goldberg, United States permanent delegate to the UN.
These were men in key positions to influence the president on
foreign policy. There were also prominent American Jews outside
official positions who had regular access to the president, even in
times of crisis: banker Abraham Feinberg, Universal Pictures president Arthur Krim and his wife Mathilde were among those who had
the president's ear.[38] Frequent telephone calls from the president to
Mrs Krim took place on the weekend before the outbreak of war.[39]

Eban, in accordance with his instructions, told the president that,
although he had originally come to Washington to discuss the Straits
of Tiran problem, an even greater issue was now at stake: the very
existence of Israel. With regard to the Straits, he reminded Johnson
of the pledges given ten years earlier and said that by closing the
Straits Nasser had, in the Israeli view, already committed an act of
aggression. Israel had only delayed reacting to it because of messages
from Washington and they now looked to see whether or not the
United States had the will and the determination to open the
Straits.[40]

In reply, President Johnson pointed out that he had already
declared that closing the Gulf of Aqaba was an illegal arbitrary
action. But to help Israel he had to convince the American cabinet,
Congress and public that Israel had been wronged for no fault of its
own or of the United States. He was at work on this but it would
take time. The United Nations must first be seen to be ineffective.
Then action must be coordinated with the British, who were willing,
and with other nations. His prerogative did not extend to saying that
an attack on Israel was an attack on the United States. His experts
did not assess the danger of an Egyptian attack on Israel as imminent. Israel could afford to wait. He gave Eban an aide-mémoire
which read:

Regarding the Straits we plan to pursue vigorously the measures which
can be taken by maritime nations to assure that the Straits and the Gulf
remain open to free and innocent passage of all nations. I must emphasize the necessity for Israel not to make itself responsible for the
initiation of hostilities. Israel will not be alone unless it decides to do it
alone. We cannot imagine that Israel will make this decision.[41]

Eban went away disappointed that Johnson had not undertaken to
actually organize the proposed naval task force.[42] The president's
silence on this point (though Eban did not stress it when he reported
to the Israeli cabinet), confirmed by a conversation on 31 May
between Brigadier Meir Amit, the head of *Mossad* (the Israeli intelligence service), and American Secretary of Defense McNamara,[43]
was sufficient to persuade the Israeli cabinet that a diplomatic
solution to Israel's dilemma was not swiftly available and that Israel
should therefore resort to force.[44] (McNamara was perhaps not the
ideal person for Amit to consult, since, it will be remembered, the
Pentagon, obsessed with Vietnam, had opposed the British proposal
for an international naval force put forward by George Thomson.)
Levi Eshkol, the Israeli prime minister and defence minister, had in
any case to bear in mind that when he had met the general staff on
28 May to explain the need for a further short delay in opening
hostilities, he had found some of his generals unhappy about any
Western plan to reopen the Straits of Tiran, on the grounds that this
was something that Israel should do itself.[45]

The good ship *Dolphin*

While Eban had been on his journey to the three capitals, Israel had
embarked on an unusual enterprise which until recently has had
some elements of mystery about it. On 25 May 1967, of the men
called to the colours as part of the Israeli mobilization, 60 who had
experience as seamen were segregated from their companions and
put on board an El Al airliner at Lydda Airport. They were flown to
East Africa and reached the port of Massawa on 27 May. There they
found a Greek cargo ship, the *Arion*, which had just been purchased

by the Israeli shipping line Zim and was being renamed the *Dol-phin*. Twenty-five of the 60 Israeli seamen replaced its Greek crew and loaded a cargo of cotton, iron, rubber and frozen meat. They also repainted the ship with the new name.[46]

The *Dolphin* was ordered to sea on 30 May, but lay off Massawa without orders to proceed further. Its crew had naturally come to the conclusion that they were to sail the *Dolphin* to Sharm al-Shaikh as a 'test ship'.[47] If it was there fired on, the Egyptians would have begun the war.

This was also the conclusion I had reached in London when I heard of the change of ownership and name. On the basis of it, and of the calculated sailing time from Massawa to Sharm al-Shaikh, I forecast to American officials during the prime minister's visit to Washington that in my view the war would begin on 3 to 5 June, as against the fortnight's delay for which they were hoping. The fore-cast turned out to be accurate, but largely serendipitous. The *Dolphin* in fact lay off Massawa until after Sharm al-Shaikh had been captured by the Israeli army. On 8 June 1967 it was ordered to proceed to Elath and cleared the Straits of Tiran on 10 June, flying the Israeli flag, to the cheers of the Israelis then occupying Sharm al-Shaikh.[48]

This was altogether a somewhat peculiar episode. It had seemed to observers, including myself, that it must be important for the Israelis to manoeuvre the Egyptians into firing the first shot of the war, a point to which, it will be remembered, de Gaulle had attached great importance. Yet they failed to use the *Dolphin* for this pur-pose. It had in fact not been usual for vessels flying the Israeli flag to sail to Elath during the decade from 1957 to 1967. The trade with Israel was conducted under other flags. Why then had the Israelis chosen to prepare a cargo ship on their own register and flying their own flag on this occasion? Was it possible that the intention was to deceive the Egyptians, who must also have learnt of the conversion of the *Arion* to the *Dolphin* at Massawa, into believing that there would be no Israeli attack upon them until after the *Dolphin* had reached Sharm al-Shaikh? If so, it would have been a deep-laid plot, but the Israelis seem never to have claimed credit for such a stratagem.[49]

Fresh light has now been thrown upon the episode by revelations in the course of a 1992 conference held to mark the 25th anniversary of the 1967 war at the State Department's Foreign Affairs Institute, attended by representatives of the former Soviet Union, Egypt, Israel, Jordan, Syria, the United States and the United Nations, most of whom had been participants in the 1967 crisis. At this exceptional gathering, two speakers alluded to the *Dolphin*. William Quandt reported that on 2 June 1967, Ephraim Evron had asked Walt Rostow at the White House what the Americans would think if there were a probe by an Israeli ship, on which the Egyptians opened fire, causing the Israelis to strike back. Would the Americans recognize this as Israel's legitimate right of self-defence under Article 51 of the United Nations Charter? Rostow said he could give no answer, but would report Evron's enquiry to the president.[50]

Then on 3 June Meir Amit, on his return from his trip to Washington, attended a meeting of the Israeli Committee for Defence and Security, at which it was decided to attack Egypt. Recounting this crucial committee meeting, he said:

> I was a bit lenient: I said, let's do something before, let's send a ship, it would take a few hours and let them shoot first, let them fire the first shot. Dayan said no, if we are alone, we have to do it alone, we cannot be dependent on any chance that might or might not happen.[51]

The committee's decision was confirmed by the Israeli cabinet the following morning and the war began the next day. It is therefore clear that use of the *Dolphin* in the Gulf of Aqaba as a final *casus belli* was in at least Mossad's mind up to the last stages of the preparations for war, but was then ruled out by Israeli ministers, led by the minister for defence.

A cabinet memorandum

In London, George Brown thought it wise to sum up the position reached up to 29 May by submitting a memorandum to the cabinet.[52] It covered a long paper by officials, setting out Britain's interests and much other relevant information, some of it in three annexes. It is worth quoting some extracts from this memorandum and its enclosure. Brown said:

> I conclude that while it is possible that Israel might restore free passage through the Gulf by her own military action, the greater risk is of an Arab/Israel war escalating. We ought therefore to contribute what we can within our resources to prevent such a war happening.

> The Israelis will only be deterred from acting if they can be reasonably assured of an international settlement that keeps the Straits open for at least their oil supplies. And international action must from their point of view seem likely to be both swift and effective.

> It was this sense of urgency that led the cabinet to authorise contingency naval planning on an 'ad referendum' basis with the Americans and preliminary diplomatic consultations with other maritime powers about asserting the international interest in keeping the Straits open. ...

> The contingency naval preparations with countries other than America ought also to proceed speedily if the possibility of multilateral escort forces is to be a credible element in a settlement. It may be that the international task force may never need to be activated. But its practicability is an essential factor in deterring both immediate war and in producing a final peaceful settlement that will not involve either Israel or Britain and other countries in a surrender of their essential interests.

Brown's memorandum referred his colleagues to the paper by officials to describe these interests and emphasized that there was no policy open to them that would altogether avoid putting them at risk. Their only choice was of the policy that would endanger them least and for the shortest time. He went on:

There are great risks whatever we do (and in doing nothing) but I conclude that it will be wisest to persist with the course on which we are already set. This means pursuing our efforts at the United Nations for a suitable Security Council resolution and at the same time go ahead with the planning of practical multilateral means of keeping the Straits of Tiran open.

It is also worth summarizing Annex 2 to the officials' paper on the practicalities of naval planning. It calculated that an escort force consisting of three escorts, four mine counter-measure vessels (it was believed, wrongly, that Nasser had mined the Straits) and one supporting tanker could reach the area by 7 June. If a guided missile destroyer were to be included in the force, it could arrive at Aden within six days. However, the fact that preparations were being made would inevitably become public knowledge.

It was on 30 May 1967 that Britain's efforts came to the knowledge of U Thant. He subsequently wrote in his memoirs:

On that day very significant developments took place outside the Security Council. Backed by the United States, Britain was reported to be taking the initiative in rallying support for the principle of freedom of passage for all ships through the Strait of Tiran, which leads into the Gulf of Aqaba. Ralph Bunche told me that he had heard from a 'British source' that London was consulting several maritime nations (including Norway, Sweden, Liberia, Ghana, Canada and Japan) on possible moves to assert the right of passage through the Strait.[53]

The prime minister's talks with Pearson and Johnson

Harold Wilson began his journey to Ottawa and Washington, to play the hand dealt to him by his cabinet. In Ottawa, which he visited on 1 June 1967, there was agreement by Prime Minister Lester Pearson on the idea of a declaration by the maritime powers, but opposition to any contingency planning for the use of force. Indeed there was even a hint that Canada might prefer to make a unilateral declaration about freedom of transit through the Gulf of

Aqaba, rather than participate in a multilateral declaration. After all, as Pearson pointed out, no Canadian shipping used the Gulf.[54]

Wilson, who had been originally invited to Canada to visit Expo '67 in Montreal (designed to commemorate the centenary of Canada's Confederation), cancelled that engagement in view of the Middle East crisis and flew on next morning to Washington.

The talks in Washington were far more crucial and had been carefully prepared. Michael Palliser, the prime minister's assistant private secretary from the Foreign Office, had gone to Washington four days ahead of the principal party to sound out the White House, the State Department and the Pentagon. He put his findings into a minute to greet the prime minister's arrival.[55] It covered a variety of subjects, but principally the Middle East. Interestingly, Palliser noted that the 'alacrity' of Britain's response to the Egypt–Israel situation had raised its stock in Washington from a low level (due, though he did not need to say so, to the United Kingdom's unwillingness to send troops to Vietnam) to a 'quasi-renewal of the happy spirit of the "special relationship"'. George Brown's initiative over the Gulf of Aqaba had at least achieved that much. (Palliser's minute is contained in Appendix B.)

A brief for President Johnson's talk with Wilson was prepared by Dean Rusk. On the Middle East, it recommended that the president should:

— Express appreciation for British willingness to play [a] direct and active role in [the] crisis.

— Tell him US–UK contingency planning for various eventualities should continue.

— Seek his views on [the] Soviet attitude.

— Sound him out as to [the] best means [of] breaking [the] impasse on [the] Straits of Tiran.[56]

The Johnson–Wilson talks of 2 June 1967, as reported by Wilson to the foreign secretary by telegram,[57] bore out Palliser's finding that

Washington was undecided on policy towards the Egypt–Israel imbroglio. Johnson (clearly with Vietnam in mind) was insistent that any use of American forces must be fully cleared with Congress and that any American action must have multilateral backing. He wished the United Kingdom to take the lead in the United Nations. His advisers thought that the whole of the following week would be available for these preliminary moves, though the president himself (rightly as it turned out) feared that Israel might act 'in a day or two'. Some military planning would be undertaken by British and American experts in Washington. Wilson suspected that more of this had already been done by the Americans than Johnson had admitted to him. (The text of Wilson's telegram is contained in Appendix C.)

There is no trace of any record by President Johnson of his talks with Wilson.[58] Clearly the occasion bulked much larger in British than in American eyes.

Parallel with the prime minister's meeting with the president, there was a meeting at the White House between British officials, led by Sir Burke Trend (secretary of the cabinet) and Sir Patrick Dean (British ambassador to the United States), with myself present, and a powerful United States team which included Dean Rusk (secretary of state), Robert McNamara (secretary of defense) and Henry Fowler (secretary of the Treasury).

The meeting covered much of the same ground as that between the prime minister and president, but it also ranged somewhat wider. In particular it speculated on the outcome of an Arab–Israeli war, with both British and Americans predicting an Israeli victory. The Americans reported an Israeli estimate of three or four days for victory over Egypt in Sinai, as against their own prediction of seven to ten days of bloody conflict. Rusk even spoke of his nightmare of an Arab victory, with the United States having to face the danger of the Israelis being swept into the sea, whereas McNamara capped this with his own nightmare of an Israeli victory which brought in the Russians. The British reaction was that both nightmares underlined the need for further efforts to prevent the outbreak of war.[59] (The record of this meeting is contained in Appendix D.)

The prime minister and his team flew on to New York for talks with U Thant and the Danish president of the Security Council, but these conversations achieved little. U Thant had already taken some personal steps to avoid, or at least delay, war. He had visited President Nasser in Cairo on 23 May to urge non-belligerency and had cabled him on 30 May. In that telegram he had said:

> I now appeal to you, Mr. President, as I am appealing to Prime Minister Eshkol and to all concerned to exercise the utmost constraint at this critical juncture. In particular, without asking any commitment from you, or indeed any reply, may I express the hope that for the next two weeks from the receipt of this message there will be no interference with non-Israeli shipping seeking passage through the Straits of Tiran. In this regard, I should advise you that in any case it is my understanding that in the normal course of events no Israeli ship is likely to seek passage through the Straits of Tiran in the next fortnight. [He did not know about the *Dolphin*.] Indeed, according to the best information available to me, no ship flying the flag of Israel has in fact sought passage through the Straits in the last two and a half years. I can assure Your Excellency that I personally, and the international community in general, would greatly appreciate such a gesture by you.[60]

It was a potentially valuable proposal, but it came too late to have a decisive influence on the course of events. U Thant may by this time have been rather sorry that he had insisted on 'all or nothing', rather than accepting Egypt's original request to withdraw UNEF from the Egyptian–Israeli armistice line only, leaving it in place at Sharm al-Shaikh and the Gaza Strip.

Outbreak of war

Wilson thus returned disappointingly empty handed to London on 4 June 1967, though still with some hope that there might be a fortnight more available for Anglo-American planning and diplomacy.

He was awakened the next morning with the news that the Arab–Israeli war had broken out.[61]

In fact the Israeli government had originally fixed 25 May as D-Day, but had put the date back to see whether the Americans would really act swiftly to open the Straits of Tiran.[62] Disappointment on this score and the economic difficulty of maintaining full mobilization for any length of time,[63] together with the appointment of the hawkish[64] General Moshe Dayan as defence minister, had finally fixed the choice as the morning of 5 June.[65]

It is possible that fears that the Egyptians might have been planning to bomb Dimona, the Israelis' nuclear reactor (Israel was then in the final stages of producing nuclear weapons with the fissionable material from Dimona), may also have played a part in the decision.[66] Reconnaissance flights by Egyptian MiG21s had been seen over Dimona on 17 May and 26 May, and on the latter occasion Rabin had informed Eshkol that he had 'peculiar and worrisome' intelligence indications that the Egyptians might be intending to bomb 'very important sites'. General Ezer Weizman had also warned Eshkol that day that all indications suggested that there might be an imminent Egyptian air attack against 'air bases and Dimona', unless Israel preempted such an attack immediately.[67]

Israel thus frustrated all Britain's (and the United States's) in the end over-slow efforts to avert the war. Given more time, the British efforts to reopen the Straits of Tiran might perhaps have succeeded. By 4 June 1967 eight countries had agreed to making a new declaration of the right of freedom of navigation in the Gulf of Aqaba: the United Kingdom, the United States, Israel, Belgium, the Netherlands, Iceland, Australia and New Zealand. There were good hopes that five more might have joined them: Canada, West Germany, Portugal, Panama and Argentina. However, only four countries had agreed to the use of force if necessary: apart from the United Kingdom and the United States (and of course Israel), the two others were the Netherlands and Australia.[68] At the 1992 retrospective conference on the 1967 war, Eugene Rostow declared: 'I believe, despite the difficulties created by the Vietnam War and Congress, the president would have gone ahead with the naval force,' but he made it clear that, 'that's a matter of, simply, faith'. Interestingly, he recounted that Golda Meir had shared his view. She had told him: 'You know, I will go to my grave believing that President Johnson would have done it.'[69]

Postscript

There is one sequel to this story which deserves mention. When, in 1971, Harold Wilson published his record of these events, he took some trouble to refute a press story about Britain's part in the war.[70] He recalled that nearly three years after the war was over, the *Daily Mail* had published 'a sensational story alleging that George Brown and I had sought to intervene, with British forces, in the Six-Day War'. The press story claimed that following the Israeli attack on Egyptian airfields, the British cabinet had been called to hear a 'startling proposition' that a strong naval contingent, headed by an aircraft carrier and cruisers, should proceed to the Gulf of Aqaba to open it to Israeli shipping. Cairo would then be informed that unless the war was stopped, British aircraft would bomb Egyptian targets. The purpose of the proposal was to protect British oil supplies and the Suez Canal from the threats arising from the continuation of the war. The *Daily Mail* concluded that this proposal had in fact been turned down by the cabinet, to Wilson's humiliation.

Refuting this story, Wilson wrote:

> Not one sentence, or thought, contained in the article had the remotest connection with fact. Because such legends can be believed and foul up international relations, a flat denial was issued by No. 10. This was printed by the *Daily Mail*, but the newspaper refused to retract; instead they sought to justify their story by a reference to a different point in history – though equally inaccurate. There were questions in Parliament, where Sir Alec Douglas-Home completely accepted our denial.
>
> I called in the Lord Chancellor to conduct an independent investigation, with access to all cabinet and cabinet committee minutes. His report to

me, setting out the results of his inquiry, ruled that the *Daily Mail* story was 'completely untrue' and confirmed the accuracy of the No. 10 statement. Fortunately the *Daily Mail*'s version was not believed abroad and no damage was done.[71]

This is a very surprising passage. Of course the original press story was completely inaccurate over the timing of the reported cabinet meeting and the proposed threat to Cairo of a British bombardment (which would have been pointless at a time when Israeli aircraft had already won the air war), but it is clearly a distorted account of what had in fact happened in cabinet, not in June but in May 1967. The *Daily Mail* had got hold of a leak, perhaps from a member of Wilson's 1967 cabinet or from a Ministry of Defence source, of what had then actually occurred, though some of the details it reported were wrong.

In 1970, when it was published, the story might just possibly have damaged Anglo-Arab relations as Wilson suggested, but if he wished to avoid that danger, No. 10 could have issued a simple denial (justified by the inaccuracies in the *Daily Mail* version) and left it at that. There was no need for Wilson to revert to the affair in his 1971 book and to bring out the extraordinary detail of the Lord Chancellor's inquiry. In practice it would be only another five years before Crossman published a more accurate version of these striking events. Nor did his disclosures then cause any obvious damage to Anglo-Arab relations. Indeed, many Arabs must have wished very much in retrospect that Britain had succeeded in averting a war that proved so disastrous to its Arab participants.

The British efforts to avert war were well intentioned and, if successful, would have been advantageous to Britain. They were foiled by the fact that Britain could no longer itself provide the naval force required, and by the reluctance of the United States, which had the necessary naval strength, to act without rather slow preparations designed to win Congressional approval. This resulted mainly from the American involvement in the Vietnam War. Other maritime nations, with a very few exceptions, proved unwilling to honour their promises of 1957 – France being a particularly blatant case. Israel had for a decade warned that an Egyptian blockade of Elath would bring war. Their decision that it should be they who made the preemptive strike must be adjudged to have been consistent with these warnings.

CHAPTER 4

THE 'BIG LIE'

IT IS NOT INTENDED HERE TO DESCRIBE in any detail the course of the war. It quickly resulted in a complete Israeli victory, the forces of Egypt, Jordan and Syria being utterly routed, despite the Soviet arms that the Egyptians and Syrians had acquired and in which Nasser had placed too much trust.

During the war, the United Kingdom maintained strict neutrality, initially prohibiting the export of arms to either side and attempting to universalize this policy into an international arms embargo.[1] Nevertheless it has now been confirmed from the 1967 official papers (as had been rumoured unofficially earlier[2]) that there were emergency deliveries of tank ammunition to Israel shortly before the war began. Wilson had pressed Israeli Prime Minister Eshkol to keep this secret, since public knowledge of it would clearly have been damaging to Anglo-Arab relations.[3]

Such damage did in fact occur, but for an entirely different and totally unforeseen reason. False Egyptian claims that the Israeli air force had been destroyed over Cairo (discarded long-range fuel tanks were mistakenly counted as shot-down aircraft[4]) grossly misled the Jordanians.[5] They saw on their radar at Ajlun Israeli planes returning to refuel after their raids on Egyptian airfields. These aircraft were landing in Israel from the sea since they had flown low over the Mediterranean to avoid Egyptian radar. Surprised by their numbers, the Jordanians wrongly interpreted them as British and American planes flying in from aircraft carriers or from Cyprus to fight alongside the Israelis. This misinterpretation was telephoned to Nasser by

King Hussein. The story, which was obviously invaluable in explaining away Egypt's loss of its air force, quickly became headline news on Cairo Radio and was repeated on other Arab broadcasts.[6]

There was another reason why the Arab countries engaged in the war believed in British and American collusion in the air battle. They knew that Israel had about 300 air force planes and were convinced from the intensity of the raids that they faced a much greater number of aircraft than Israel could use for attack. They misinterpreted Israeli tactics and grossly underestimated Israeli efficiency. Tactically, they could not believe that Israel would leave only 12 planes to guard their home base.[7] Nor did they realize that the Israelis had cut down their turn-around time after raids to as little as seven to ten minutes. Randolph and Winston Churchill, who had access to full information from Israeli sources, had this to say:

> Nasser knew well that by Egyptian standards, at least, the Israelis did not have a large air force. They had a total of about 300 aircraft. … Yet reports had come into him of wave upon wave of Israeli aircraft attacking some 19 of his airbases at 10-minute intervals for 2 hours and 50 minutes with scarcely a break.[8]

In his resignation speech of 9 June, Nasser declared:

> If we say now that it was a stronger blow than we expected we must say at the same time and with assurance that it was much stronger than his resources allowed. The enemy attacked at one go all the military and civil airfields in the United Arab Republic. This meant that he was relying on something more than his normal strength to protect his skies from any retaliation from us. … It can be said without fear of exaggeration that the enemy was operating an airforce three times its normal strength.[9]

The reference by Nasser to the Israeli air force being 'three times its normal strength' is significant. He was evidently basing his claim on the turn-around time of his own air force. The Israelis learnt from top secret Egyptian air force plans they captured at El Arish that the Egyptians based their plans on their aircraft being overhead their targets every three hours instead of every hour or less, as was the case with the Israeli air force. Compared with the ground turn-around time of seven to ten minutes of the Israeli air force, that of the Egyptians was more than two hours. While the Egyptians reckoned on two sorties a day per aircraft, many of the Israeli pilots flew eight, and a few even more on the Monday of the war.[10]

As early as 0437 GMT on 6 June 1967 (0737 Cairo time), the BBC Monitoring Service recorded Cairo Radio as saying:

> The Supreme Command of the armed forces in the UAR announces that it has now become quite certain that the USA and Britain are taking part in the Israeli military aggression in so far as the air operations are concerned. It has been fully proved that some British and US aircraft carriers are carrying out wide scale activities in helping Israel. On the Egyptian front, the US and British aircraft have created an air umbrella over Israel. On the Jordanian front, these aircraft are playing an actual role in the operations against the Jordanian forces, as was shown by the Jordanian radar screens which clearly showed this air activity which helps Israel. King Husayn of Jordan early this morning got in touch with President Jamal Abd an-Nasir and informed him that now he was confident that the British and US aircraft were playing a serious role in the battle. This confirmed information available from the Egyptian front. The King and the President agreed that this serious development should be announced to the entire Arab nation and that inevitably stands must be taken with regard to it.[11]

Not to be outdone, Damascus Radio at 0705 GMT on 6 June added its own (alleged) confirmatory evidence.

> An official spokesman has stated the following:

> The intensity of the enemy air raids yesterday, the control network, the observations of Syrian air pilots, and the confessions of the Zionist pilot officer Abraham (?Zilah), whose raiding aircraft was destroyed by our valiant forces – our Arab viewers saw him on Arab television yesterday – all this has confirmed that US and British aircraft in fact participated directly in the gangster state's aggression yesterday.

This Zionist pilot confessed that 17 British Vulcan bombers arrived 10 days ago at the Israeli air base at Eqron, where he worked. In his recorded confession, the Zionist pilot admitted that these 17 British aircraft had participated in yesterday's battles and bombed targets inside the Syrian Arab Republic and the UAR.[12]

Britain had to mount a major campaign to get these false stories contradicted. From his previous career, Sir Paul Gore-Booth, the permanent under-secretary at the Foreign Office, was experienced in information work: he had been director of British Information Services in the United States from 1949 to 1953. On his initiative a special diplomatic task force was set up, which entitled these stories the 'big lie' and used every available means to contradict them.[13] The Americans, of course, also denied involvement in the fighting. Two important platforms for such denials were the United Nations and the House of Commons, and both of these were used to the full.

On the afternoon of 6 June, Harold Wilson made a statement to the Commons. He said:

> A most serious development has been the deliberate spreading by the United Arab Republic Government of entirely false accusations that British and American aircraft have taken part in the fighting on the side of Israel. It has been announced that President Nasser has announced that he will, in retaliation, close the Suez Canal to navigation. President Aref of Iraq is also reported to have said that he has ordered a cessation of the pumping of oil to the Mediterranean for the same reason and there have also been reports that the Kuwait Government have forbidden oil exports to British and American destinations.
>
> Her Majesty's Government have already categorically denied this monstrous story, and all our Ambassadors in the Arab countries have been instructed to make clear to the local governments that this is a malicious and mischievous invention. One story alleges that aircraft from British aircraft carriers have taken part in the fighting. During the past week the only British aircraft carriers in the area have been HMS *Victorious*, which has been at Malta, and HMS *Hermes*, which has been at Aden,

each over 1000 miles away. In view of these incontrovertible facts, we are calling upon the Arab Governments not to disrupt commercial arrangements which are as much in their interests as ours on the basis of such false statements.[14]

In the United Nations Security Council, the United States permanent delegate, Arthur Goldberg, was able to make an American refutation on 6 June 1967. He told the Council that allegations that United States aircraft had been involved in the hostilities were totally without foundation.

> I take the opportunity in the Security Council on the complete authority of the United States Government to deny them categorically without any ifs, ands or buts. Indeed, yesterday morning, 5 June, within hours after first hearing such charges, my Government denied them in a formal statement issued by the Department of Defense as follows:

>> There have been reports that United States aircraft from aircraft carriers assigned to the Sixth Fleet have flown to Israel airfields. Other reports have stated that Sixth Fleet aircraft have participated in air activity elsewhere in the area of conflict. All such reports are erroneous. All Sixth Fleet aircraft are and have been several hundred miles from the area of conflict.

He pointed out the danger of such false charges in a highly inflammable situation. They had been used to incite mob violence against American diplomatic and other installations in several Arab states.

> With this in mind, I am authorized to announce in this Council and to propose two concrete measures. The United States is prepared, first, to cooperate in an immediate impartial investigation by the United Nations of these charges, and to offer all facilities to the United Nations in that investigation; and second, as part of or in addition to such an investigation, the United States is prepared to invite United Nations personnel aboard our aircraft carriers in the Mediterranean today, tomorrow, or at the convenience of the United Nations, to serve as impartial observers of the activities of our planes from our official records and from the log that

each ship carries. These observers will, in addition, be free to interview air crews on these carriers without inhibition, so as to determine their activities during the days in question.[15]

This was an offer that must have impressed most of the delegates who heard it. Goldberg said that it would remain open throughout the period of the crisis and as long as the vessels concerned were in the Eastern Mediterranean.

Later in the same day, the United Kingdom permanent delegate, Lord Caradon, addressed the Council on the same theme:

> Mr. President, I must first ask your indulgence if I make a short state-ment on a matter of great importance to my government and my country. Speaking today in the House of Commons, my Prime Minister referred to false accusations that British aircraft have taken part in the fighting on the side of Israel. These are the words that my Prime Min-ister used: [already quoted above].
>
> I have today, Mr. President, addressed to you a letter on this important matter dealing with these lies which have been circulated in various forms here in New York. I shall read out this short letter, if I may, be-cause it is necessary that these matters should be finally disposed of. The letter reads as follows:
>
>> Her Majesty's Government have been shocked by reports emanating from the Middle East and carried by official news media alleging that British aircraft have taken part in the recent fighting in the Mid-dle East on the side of Israel. These reports are malicious falsehoods. There is no grain of truth in them.
>
> It is the policy of Her Majesty's Government to avoid taking sides in the conflict in the Middle East and they have done everything they can to bring about a cease-fire as soon as possible. As stated by my Secretary of State in the House of Commons yesterday, all British forces in the area have been under the strictest instructions not to become involved in any way.[16]

Needless to say, these two statements did not inhibit the Arab delegates from repeating their allegations to the Security Council, but they undermined the likelihood of any wider international belief in the stories.

The Israelis were, for their part, furious to have their victories attributed to non-existent British and American support. They quickly issued their own denial. On the evening of 6 June Israel Radio broadcast in its Arabic service the following statement:

> Since yesterday evening, and throughout today, the Egyptian propa- ganda trumpets – which have been joined by the propaganda trumpets of the Arab countries which were dragged into the aggressive Egyptian adventure – have devoted all their efforts to involving American and British forces in the war and creating the impression that the Israeli De- fence Army's sweeping victory over the aggressive land and air forces was not the result of the Israeli Army's superiority over the aggressors, its magnificent tactics and unprecedented war capability, but the result of participation in the war by the US and British Air Forces.

The statement went on to make it clear that this claim was 'a lie and a violation of the truth':

> If the Egyptian authorities and the authorities which join them in this lie were truthful, they would have presented evidence on Arab television by showing the American and British aircraft, since they claim to have shot down over 150 raiding aircraft. This lie is ridiculous. We trust that the Arab masses will not believe it. We also trust that the world will not consider it to be anything more than a mere claim deserving pity.[17]

President Johnson made a personal effort to enlist Soviet help in refuting the false charges. For the first time in its history, the 'hot line' between Moscow and Washington had been brought into serious action during the Arab–Israeli crisis. In replying to a message from Soviet Prime Minister Kosygin, President Johnson used the hot line as he describes in his memoirs:

I mentioned the false Arab allegation in my answer to Kosygin over the hot line. I told him that since his intelligence knew where our carriers and planes were, I hoped he would emphasize the facts to Cairo.[18]

This appeal brought no specific response, though it was noticeable to those capable of reading between the lines that Soviet charges of support for Israel by the United States and Britain were always couched in general terms and never alleged intervention in combat by British and American aircraft. Those who attended to details could draw their own conclusions.

British, American and Israeli denials, and the lack of any physical evidence to support the Arab allegations, were soon able to convince non-Arab nations that there was no truth in the charges of collusion. But the Arabs refused to abandon their story. It was necessary for George Brown, when he attended the fifth emergency session of the United Nations General Assembly later in June, to revert to the denial of the charges. Speaking after the Soviet delegate, he said early in his speech:

> I must say, in all frankness, that we have been subjected here to an amazing amount of double talk.

> I read very carefully the speech which Mr. Kosygin made on Monday. ... He made a number of specific charges against the United Kingdom. I heard them repeated yesterday and I want to answer them one by one.

> First, Mr. Kosygin said, and I quote his words:

>> Israel has enjoyed outside support from certain imperialist circles. ... these powerful circles made statements and took practical actions which might have been interpreted by Israeli extremists ... as direct encouragement to commit acts of aggression.

> In this context he went on to refer to the movements of British naval and air forces to bring pressure to bear upon Arab States.

> I notice that Mr. Kosygin did not say that there was direct participation by British forces in the fighting. He knows that this cannot possibly be

true. He can verify – and no doubt has – the facts from his own sources. There were, after all, rather considerable Soviet naval forces in the Mediterranean at the very same time. Those who put around these falsehoods must have known, must now know, that they were and are totally untrue. Nevertheless, throughout the fighting, and since, they were repeated over and over again by Cairo Radio and by other radio stations all over the Middle East.

Brown doubted whether there was anyone hearing him (obviously including the Arabs) who accepted any of these allegations. He also offered evidence to refute the stories.

We for our part have said that we would welcome intensive investigation by the United Nations, and this offer still stands. We have taken an un-precedented step: we have placed the log books of our ships in the library of the House of Commons and they are there now for consulta-tion by anybody who wishes to consult them.

Brown ended by recalling the friendship that the British govern-ment, and he personally, had had with the Arab states, and regretting the damage that these false charges had done to it. He called for a renewal of the friendship now that the false charges had been refuted.[19]

This intensive programme of denials finally bore fruit. The Jordanians were prevailed upon to admit that their radar report had been erroneous and this undermined the basis for the lie, even in the Arab world.[20] And eventually, in an interview published in *Look* magazine, President Nasser himself admitted that his accusation had been based on suspicion and faulty information.[21] He had already admitted this confidentially in the speech he had made at the Arab Summit Conference in Khartoum in August 1967.[22]

Arab measures against Britain

Meanwhile, however, the allegations had naturally been widely believed in many Arab countries, where there were mob attacks on British and American embassies and consulates.[23] On 5 and 6 June,

Iraq, Syria and the Sudan broke off diplomatic relations with the United Kingdom (Egypt, Algeria and Mauritania had already been out of relations because of disapproval by the Organization of African Unity of Britain's policy towards Rhodesia). In Baghdad, for instance, the British ambassador, Richard Beaumont, was summoned to the Iraqi Ministry of Foreign Affairs on the morning of 5 June, accused of aid to Israel by the Royal Air Force and given 48 hours for himself and his staff to leave the country. They drove in convoy into Iran, escorted to the frontier by Iraqi military vehicles, and flew back to London from Tehran. Ironically their plane refuelled in Israel.[24]

There were also serious economic consequences for Britain. As George Brown had foreseen, one of the effects of the war had been the closure of the Suez Canal. With Israeli troops on the east bank of the Canal, it remained closed until June 1975, which seriously damaged Britain's trade.[25] Shipping, including much British shipping (the United Kingdom was one of the principal Canal users), had for eight years to use the longer Cape route, at considerably higher freight charges.

In early June 1967, again because of the 'big lie', oil exports to the United Kingdom and the United States were prohibited by Algeria, Kuwait, Libya, Saudi Arabia, and even Bahrain, Qatar and Abu Dhabi, and the ban was not lifted until the Khartoum Summit of Arab countries on 29 August 1967.[26]

Although this oil ban lasted less than three months, it caused considerable distortion in the pattern of supplies to the United Kingdom. Thanks to the efficiency of the major oil companies in redistributing deliveries among their customers, there was no overall problem in meeting British needs. Petrol rationing coupons were printed but did not need to be issued. The main switch of supplies was not to the western hemisphere producers, but within the Persian Gulf, as Iran replaced the Arab countries. Kuwaiti deliveries fell from £92.7 million in 1966 to £75.6 million in 1967, Iraqi deliveries from £65.6 million in 1966 to £24.1 million in 1967, Qatari deliveries from £16.8 million in 1966 to £4.3 million in 1967, Abu Dhabi deliveries from £11.1 million in 1966 to £5.9 million in 1967, and Bahraini deliveries from £5.6 million in 1966 to £2.9 million in 1967. Interestingly, Saudi and Libyan deliveries rose in 1967 (Libya was of course on the western side of the Suez Canal), and the main gainer was Iran, with an increase from £38.2 million in 1966 to £136.7 million in 1967.[27]

Iranian oil was rather more expensive to produce than some of the Arab oil, particularly that from Kuwait, so there was some extra cost to the United Kingdom as a result of the switch. There was also some damage to the profits of British producers, particularly British Petroleum, so the Treasury suffered loss from reduced corporation tax. But the main adverse effect, shared by other European countries, was from the extra cost of shipments by the longer route round Africa at a time when there were few really large tankers available. With the building of super-tankers, this loss gradually reduced, but it was considerable in 1967.

Harold Wilson blamed this for the devaluation of sterling which followed five months later. He wrote in his memoirs:

> The economic consequences of this June week were extremely serious for Britain. The closure of the Suez Canal alone, it was authoritatively estimated, was costing Britain £20 millions a month on our balance of payments. No less serious was the loss of Middle East oil. We had to seek to replace this from other areas at a higher price and, in the main, at much higher freights.

Wilson claimed that before the war British exports, balance of payments and sterling had all been strong. There had even been a balance of payments surplus in late 1966 and early 1967. In May 1967 the bank rate had been reduced to 5½ per cent, the lowest figure for two and a half years. But the war had wrecked Britain's economic recovery:

> The Middle East crisis of June 1967 was the biggest contributing factor to the devaluation which came five months later. ... It was to be two

years more and at heavy cost – economic, social and political – before we
were able to regain our surplus position.[28]

In this analysis Wilson was, in fact, minimizing other contributing influences and the fact that, contrary to his account, sterling had
been relatively weak enough before the war to have been one of the
subjects planned for discussion between him and President Johnson
during his Washington visit in early June.[29] Nevertheless the effects
on Britain of the Canal closure were certainly severe and it was
ironic that the United Kingdom, which had tried so hard to avert the
threat of the third Arab–Israeli war, should have been damaged so
very badly by its outcome. This damage, clearly foreseen by George
Brown, was his justification for the change of policy represented by
his strenuous, though eventually unsuccessful, efforts to prevent the
closure of the Gulf of Aqaba to shipping bound to and from Elath.

Thus, although the war lasted only six days and although the
United Kingdom played no part in it, Britain suffered lasting damage from the false accusations of collusion with Israel, believed in the
Arab countries largely as a result of memories of 1956. The ill effects
included not only the devaluation of sterling, partly caused by heavy
freight charges for shipments round South Africa, but also a loss of
diplomatic relations with many Arab countries. It was a major task
for the Foreign Office, and for George Brown personally, to counter
this situation and to restore the United Kingdom's standing in the
Arab world. That this was in the event achieved remarkably quickly
will be seen in Chapter 6.

CHAPTER 5

POSTWAR POLICIES

ISRAEL, IMMEDIATELY AFTER THE END OF THE WAR, was faced with the problem of forming a policy on how to deal with the extensive territories it had occupied: Sinai and the Gaza Strip, the Golan Heights, and the West Bank including East Jerusalem. Opinions were not surprisingly divided within the now broadly based government of national unity, although all parties were unanimous that there should be no repetition of the 1956 withdrawal under international pressure. Fortunately for Israel, it was already clear from the Security Council arguments over ceasefire resolutions, and was rapidly confirmed, that the United States would this time be supporting Israel's contention that withdrawal must be balanced by Arab concessions amounting to the making of peace with Israel.

As early as 13 June Eshkol held a meeting with leading ministers to formulate a policy on the territorial aspects of peace terms for Egypt, Syria and Jordan. It was surprisingly rapidly concluded that, against adequate Arab concessions directly negotiated, Israeli troops would be withdrawn from Sinai and the Golan Heights to the international borders between what had been mandatory Palestine and Egypt and Syria. This would leave the Gaza Strip in Israeli hands. As for Jordan, there should be withdrawal from the heavily populated areas of the West Bank, but the details of this were left vague.

Egypt's concessions were to include:

1. freedom of navigation in the Gulf of Aqaba and through the Straits of Tiran;

2. freedom of navigation in the Suez Canal;

3. overflight rights in the Gulf of Aqaba and over the Straits of Tiran;

4. demilitarization of the Sinai Peninsula.

Syria's concessions were to include:

1. demilitarization of the Golan Heights;

2. non-interference with the flow of water from the sources of the River Jordan to Israel.

These terms were processed through the Israeli government machinery and were agreed unanimously in cabinet on 19 June: it was decided to defer a decision on the precise terms to be applied to Jordan. They were then communicated to Eban, who had gone to New York in preparation for United Nations discussions, and he was authorized to communicate them to the Americans for onward transmission to the Arabs. He did so to Dean Rusk on 21 June, who according to Eban received the communication with amazement at its generosity. However, the Egyptians and Syrians were less impressed. They rejected the terms completely, demanding that Israeli withdrawal must be unconditional. The Israelis did not withdraw their offers, but decided to keep them secret from the public. That, as time went on, left them open to second thoughts.[1]

The fifth emergency session of the UN General Assembly

On 20 June 1967 George Brown flew to New York to attend the special session summoned to debate the situation following the Arab–Israeli war, on which the Security Council had failed to pass a definitive resolution. He took with him a team of officials, including the permanent under-secretary of state, Sir Paul Gore-Booth, who was the expert on combating the 'big lie' (see Chapter 4); Sir Harold Beeley, a former ambassador to Egypt; and me, then assistant under-secretary of state for Middle East affairs. In New York, this team was joined by Lord Caradon and his staff.

On the flight to New York Brown examined for the first time the speech drafted for him by officials (Eastern Department in consultation with United Nations Department). He summoned me and voiced his displeasure. His complaint was that the speech, which was (deliberately) full of admirable but relatively uncontroversial statements, would have been suitable enough for delivery by an official. But he was the foreign secretary and must say something of which the press and parliament would take notice. He demanded a redraft with more life in it.

I replied that it would be possible, for instance, to strengthen the section on the unacceptability under the United Nations Charter of territorial gains made by conquest. There could also be a paragraph on Jerusalem, where, because of the United Nations partition plan of 1947, the British government had never recognized the right of either Israel or Jordan to claim sovereignty. But this would produce a speech highly objectionable to the Israelis. I was told nevertheless to redraft on these lines and to clear the amended speech with Beeley, in case he had comments. This was done and Brown accepted the redraft.[2]

Caradon had already put down Brown's name to speak early in the debate. He began his speech by dealing with the 'big lie' (in the passage quoted in Chapter 4). The remainder of his speech followed as redrafted. The crucial elements of the redraft were paragraphs 15 and 16, the key sentences being: 'In my view, it follows from the words in the Charter that war should not lead to territorial aggrandisement' and 'I say very solemnly to the Government of Israel that, if they purport to annex the Old City or legislate for its annexation, they will be taking a step which will isolate them not only from world opinion but will also lose them the support which they have.' In effect therefore, Brown was calling upon the Israelis to withdraw from all the territories they had just conquered, including East Jerusalem.

There were some balancing passages in the speech, notably 'the right of all States to exist in true dignity and real freedom' and their 'ability to earn their living in assured peace', plus 'the right of free and innocent passage through international waterways for the ships of all nations', but withdrawal and Jerusalem were the crux of it.[3] (A fairly full extract from Brown's speech is contained in Appendix E.)

In deciding, without reference to the cabinet or the prime minister, to make such a pro-Arab speech, Brown may have been partly influenced not only by his own inclinations but also by a personal telegram sent to him during the war by Lord Caradon. This had said:

It may be worth making the point that we here are in a good position to maintain working relations with the Arabs. ...

2. I have very friendly personal relations with them all including El Kony (UAR). When I told him today that we must keep our lines open here he warmly thanked me. And El Farra (Jordan) whose home in Khan Yunis has been overrun in the Israeli advance is an old friend.

3. We must start rebuilding bridges with them.[4]

However this may be, the reaction to Brown's speech was significant. There was a buzz of discussion in the Arab delegations, and the Israelis left the Assembly immediately, obviously to discuss counter-tactics. Brown performed the usual courtesy of sitting through the speech that followed and then also left the Assembly, with me and other members of his team. To his slight consternation Brown immediately ran into the Israeli delegation, who had not gone back to their office but had taken the nearest block of chairs in the ante-room. Among them was Golda Meir, the former Israeli foreign minister, now secretary-general of the Alignment Party, who was an old friend of Brown's from meetings of the Socialist International. With only a second's hesitation he went across to Golda Meir and kissed her on the cheek, as had been his normal practice. I was the only other member of the British delegation close enough to hear her one-word comment, which, interestingly, was 'Judas'. Brown said nothing and led the way on to the United Kingdom delegation's offices.

It is notable that, in the long debate that followed, none of the Arab delegates made any comment at all on Brown's speech. They were still adhering publicly to their charges of British and American collusion with Israel, and evidently found it incompatible to say anything favourable at that time about a British speech. But most of them spoke well of it privately in the corridors and in the bilateral discussions that Brown had with Arab foreign ministers. This was true of the foreign ministers or other spokesmen of, successively, Tunisia, Iraq, the United Arab Republic, Lebanon, Libya and Morocco.[5] Nor did any of them mention the 'big lie', which, as Brown had said in his speech, none of them any longer believed (though they did not actually bring themselves to admit as much).

Brown had two meetings with the Israeli delegation, who were still critical of his speech but had calmed down a great deal. They had no doubt come to the conclusion that nothing said in the United Nations was going to determine their policy, and that, as long as they had United States support, Britain's attitude was of minor importance. Moreover, they knew that they had a friend in Harold Wilson.

Reactions to the speech in Britain

Reports of Brown's speech caused a good deal of surprise in political circles in London, as Richard Crossman reported:

> When the Chief [Chief Whip, John Silkin, a Jew] and I had strolled back to the House we found a crowd round the tape, studying another speech by George Brown at the U.N. attacking the Israelis, telling them that they had to get out of the territories they had occupied and that they could not be allowed to have Jerusalem. When he read this John walked down to the library with me and told me that if that was our policy he would have to resign. I rang Harold [Wilson] at once and told him that this was really intolerable for the Chief and that there was bound to be a bleeding row in Cabinet next morning.[6]

In the event, the prime minister calmed things down, both in cabinet and in the Commons, and John Silkin thought better of resigning.

However, as soon as Brown returned to London from the special session, he was at once made aware that his pro-Arab speech had attracted criticism in Britain, both in parliament and more generally. The criticism came from Jewish commentators, including Jewish MPs, who (like Silkin) disapproved of the passages on withdrawal and Jerusalem, and also from right-wing Tories who had supported Eden's invasion of the Suez Canal area in 1956 and still retained their hatred of Nasser. Brown answered them all in the speech he made in the House of Commons reporting on his visit to New York:

> The speech was I think well received in the United Nations itself and in newspaper, television and radio comment in New York. I gather that it has had a more mixed reception in this country. I must emphasize that we must at all costs avoid falling into the trap of applying a double standard. Would a similar line have been taken if the war had gone the other way – if, for example, the Arab air force had struck first and if Arab armies had occupied significant parts of the territory of Israel? What would then have been said about the permanent retention of territorial gains made by conquest?

As for the status of Jerusalem, he reminded the House of the attitude of successive British governments in the past. He pointed out that a United Nations General Assembly Resolution of 9 December 1949 had provided that there should be a unified city under international control. For this reason, the British government, along with most other Western governments, had always withheld recognition of the claims to sovereignty over Jerusalem by both Jordan and Israel, pending a final settlement. This was why their embassies to Israel were not in Jerusalem but in Tel Aviv. He continued:

> I therefore went on in my speech in New York to warn the Israeli Government not to inject another complication into the situation which is already sufficiently complicated by purporting to annex the old city. ... I am not asking for a return to a divided Jerusalem. Nor do I want to fore-

cast what the arrangements may be, except to repeat what I said in New York, that any lasting settlement of which they form part must, among other things, clearly recognise the right of all states concerned to live in true dignity and true freedom.[7]

This speech was generally successful in mollifying opinion in the House of Commons and to some extent among the public, though by no means entirely.

Internationally, Brown's speech to the General Assembly contributed a great deal to the subsequent rapid improvement in Arab–British relations. For instance, Dingle Foot, an independent-minded MP (and Caradon's brother), reported to the House of Commons on a visit he had made to Cairo in October 1967:

> I came back from Cairo with the impression that not only in official circles but very widely indeed, there was a desire for *rapprochement* with this country. It was largely due to the speech made by my right hon. Friend [George Brown] at the end of the fighting last July [in fact, June]. I think that we can now feel that we are entering a new and more hopeful chapter in Anglo-Arab relations.[8]

It is often disputed that one man can have a decisive effect on international relations, especially if he is operating from a base within a second-rank power like the United Kingdom. But George Brown goes far to demonstrate the contrary. Not only by his plan for a naval force to open the Gulf of Aqaba, which had so impressed Eugene Rostow, but also by this speech to the General Assembly and later by his efforts to restore diplomatic relations with the Arab states,[9] he dominated British policy making on the Middle East in 1967 and eventually greatly improved Britain's international standing in the Arab world. It is true that his personal reputation inevitably stood a good deal lower in Israel, but that did not seriously damage the United Kingdom's overall relations with that country, since there were plenty of other Britons, including Harold Wilson, whom the Israelis knew to be sympathetic to them. On balance, Brown's speech to the fifth emergency session of the General Assembly must be regarded as very much a personal triumph during his period as foreign secretary.

The Khartoum Arab Summit Conference

Their overwhelming defeat in the June war had left the Arab countries in great disarray. Jordan and Egypt in particular were virtually bankrupt: Jordan from its loss of tourism and transit trade and Egypt from its loss of Canal revenues and the cost of rebuilding its armed forces. The whole of the Arab world was shocked and humiliated. A regrouping and reconsideration of policy was urgently needed. Thanks largely to the efforts of the Sudanese, it was decided to call a summit meeting in Khartoum.

The kings and heads of state assembled there towards the end of August 1967, and the conference opened on 30 August with the Sudanese president, Ismail El Azhari, in the chair. All the expected delegates were there except President Nouriddine Al-Atassi of Syria and President Houari Boumedienne of Algeria. The Algerian foreign minister, Abdul Aziz Bouteflika, attended the conference, but the Syrian foreign minister, who had been in Khartoum, departed on 31 August on the instructions of his government.

Before the conference opened, an agreement between Egypt and Saudi Arabia on their part in the Yemen civil war had been reached in Cairo.[10] It was confirmed in the margins of the conference at a private meeting of Nasser and King Faisal in Azhari's presence, which lasted into the early hours of 31 August.[11] It was decided to set up a three-man committee, consisting of representatives of Morocco (chosen by Saudi Arabia), Iraq (chosen by Egypt) and Sudan (mutually agreed). This would 'formulate a plan that would ensure the withdrawal of UAR troops from Yemen and ensure the stoppage of Saudi military assistance from all Yemenis'.

After this marked initial success, the conference proceeded rapidly to important conclusions. It held its last open session on 1 September, with Azhari reading out an agreed communiqué and the Sudanese prime minister proclaiming the agreed resolutions of the conference.[12] There were seven of these, of which three were of principal interest to Britain:

> Third. The Arab Kings and Heads of State agreed on the unification of their efforts in joint political and diplomatic action at the international level to the withdrawal of the aggressive Israeli forces from the occupied Arab territory after June 5th, within the framework of the basic Arab commitment and conviction which entails non-recognition of Israel, nor conciliation, nor negotiation with her, but upholding the rights of the Palestinian people to their land.
>
> Fourth. The Ministers of Finance, Economy and Petrol recommended the possibility of using the petrol as a weapon in the struggle. But the Summit Conference, after careful study, sees that the petrol export could be used as a positive weapon, which would be directed towards the consolidation of the economy of the Arab Nations that directly suffered from the aggression to help them in facing the pressures of battle.
> …
>
> Seventh. The Conference decided to speed up the liquidation of the foreign bases in the Arab Nations.

Outcome of the conference

The head of the British Interests Section in Khartoum, Norman Reddaway, sent two important telegrams to sum up the results of the conference. The first assessed the outcome as being 'as satisfactory as we can reasonably expect'.[13] From the British point of view, the decision on oil exports 'removes a serious threat'. The oil-producing states would face a heavy bill. It had been decided that Saudi Arabia would contribute annually £50 million, Kuwait £55 million and Libya £30 million, these funds going to Egypt and Jordan in monthly or quarterly tranches. Syria, having absented itself from the conference, was to get nothing. Reddaway described the badly translated third resolution as 'predictable'. (It was soon retranslated as what became known as the 'Three Noes': no recognition, no peace and no negotiations.) He suggested that the resolution on foreign bases might cause Britain some trouble in the Persian Gulf, but this proved not to be true.

His second telegram was sent after he had had time for discussions with leading Sudanese about the outcome, and referred particularly to the implications for Britain. It is worth quoting fairly fully:

> There are definite signs in the wake of the Arab Summit Conference that the consensus of opinion among the Arab leaders was to cease to treat Britain as an enemy. ...
>
> Further indications of détente are an account by a leading Sudanese journalist in the Sudan News Agency of the conference proceedings which specifically said that discussion took place on Britain's relations with the Arabs and opening the way to new relations with her on a sound basis. There was also a reference to 'the countries which were acquitted of supporting Israel'. We have checked this story with the author, Abdel Karim El Mahdi, who is very close to the Egyptians. He confirmed that although some countries favoured putting greater pressure on Britain the general view was that there was more to be gained by trying to enlist Britain's support than by continuing to lump her in with the United States. ...
>
> Our own assessment here from talking to Sudanese contacts is that:-
>
> (a) the Summit considered improving relations with the West – now that the oil weapon has been discarded – as one of the more hopeful means of putting pressure on Israel;
>
> (b) the Arabs look to Britain as the western country which (for better or worse) understands them best. They still cannot bring themselves to talk to the Americans and feel that in any case on the question of Israel they would be talking to a brick wall;
>
> (c) there is no clear idea how Britain could help but there is a disposition to feel that she could now do something.[14]

Reddaway ended this telegram with a recommendation that the secretary of state should not comment directly on the outcome of the summit but would catch the mood of the moment if he were to recapitulate the point made in his speech to the fifth emergency session of the General Assembly rejecting territorial aggrandizement through military conquest. The Foreign Office sympathized with this recommendation, but it was decided that on balance the recapitulation was not advisable in the light of the generally unsympathetic reception that Brown's speech had had in Britain.

There was an interesting addition from the British embassy in Tripoli to the conference story.[15] The Libyan foreign minister, Dr Bishti, invited the British ambassador to call and made the following comment on the conference:

> President Nasser had been moderate and subdued. He had given the Conference a detailed account of the origins of the 'big lie' (Dr Bishti's words). King Hussein had telephoned him saying that he was being attacked by four hundred Israeli aircraft, that his radar showed them to be coming from the sea and that if there were four hundred in the air 'there must be four hundred on the ground'. Since this was far more than their information of the strength of Israeli aircraft, King Hussein had deduced that help must be reaching the Israelis from outside and that the only possible source was Britain and America. On this basis the accusation against Britain and America had been put out. President Nasser left no doubt in the minds of the conference that he no longer believed the story. His account passed without comment by King Hussein.

This episode naturally aroused considerable interest in the Foreign Office. The team that had worked to counter the 'big lie' derived particular satisfaction from it.[16]

These three developments in postwar policy making were of lasting significance. The Israeli reversal of their intentions regarding the handing back of the West Bank bedevilled Jordanian efforts to reach a peaceful settlement and still to this day complicates Israeli negotiations with the Palestinians. George Brown's speech to the General Assembly was the first step in his programme of improving Britain's relations with the Arab states, and his warning to the Israelis of the dangers to them of annexing East Jerusalem, although it bore no fruit in their policy decisions, has been prophetic of their current difficulties in making peace with the Palestinians. The 'Three Noes' of the Khartoum Summit have been less long lasting in their effects, but were ever present in Arab minds in their dealings with Israel in 1967–68.

CHAPTER 6

DIPLOMATIC RELATIONS WITH ARAB COUNTRIES

IN DECEMBER 1965 a large number of African countries, including Egypt, Algeria, Sudan and Somalia, had broken off diplomatic relations with the United Kingdom. They did so at the request of the Organization of African Unity, which was protesting against Britain's failure to use force to quell the Rhodesian unilateral declaration of independence. Protecting powers were appointed, but in all cases the United Kingdom was allowed to retain some of its embassy staff as British Interests Sections working with, and in theory under, the protecting powers.

In June 1967, following the outbreak of the Arab–Israeli war and the false charges of British and American collusion with Israel, further Arab countries broke relations. Syria and Iraq did so on 5 June, and Sudan, which had meanwhile restored relations after the 1965 break, broke again on 6 June. Of these, only Sudan permitted the retention of a British Interests Section, in this case consisting of the whole of the embassy staff other than the ambassador.

Diplomatic relations with Egypt

In Egypt, where the protecting power was Canada, the British Interests Section held its own ciphers, so was able to communicate directly and secretly with the Foreign Office. The head of the Section, Fletcher, was replaced in 1967 by Robert Tesh. Official messages between the United Kingdom and Egyptian governments were transmitted in Cairo by the Canadian embassy, but the head of the British Interests Section had a wide range of unofficial contacts, including important Egyptians.[1]

Mohamed Hassanain Heikal was the editor of the leading Egyptian newspaper *al-Ahram*, and was known to be a close friend and confidant of President Nasser. On 11 April 1967 he asked Fletcher to visit him in his office. There he passed him a message from the Egyptian government to the British foreign secretary, explaining that he was doing so because the government preferred in this case to use an unofficial channel rather than the official one through the Ministry of Foreign Affairs and the Canadian embassy. The message was that the five African countries, Egypt, Algeria, Tanzania, Mauritania and Guinea, which had just been holding a meeting in Cairo on 6 April 1967, had decided to seek to resume relations with the United Kingdom on 1 July 1967. He asked that no public mention be made of this message and commented that he hoped George Brown would find the message 'good cheer' after 'his gallant defence in the House of Commons debate'.[2]

The background to this message was that the British Labour Party, which was now in office, had earlier opposed the Eden government over its Suez policy in 1956. When it came to power in 1964 it expected to benefit from this in its relations with Arab countries, especially Egypt. Moreover Brown, when in opposition, had travelled widely and made important foreign contacts, including President Nasser, whom he had visited several times and counted as a friend.[3] On becoming foreign secretary, Brown let it be widely known that if the Egyptians wished to resume diplomatic relations, they would find the door open.[4]

The Foreign Office was pleased by this message from Nasser but puzzled by some aspects of it, especially as it had heard nothing by way of corroboration from the other African countries mentioned by Heikal. But it was in any case soon rendered out of date by the June 1967 Arab–Israeli war and the 'big lie'.

On 10 September 1967 the *Sunday Times* published an article by Heikal about Anglo-Egyptian relations, tracing them from the bombardment of Alexandria in 1882 to the present day. His theme was that during the whole of that time there had never been a true dialogue between the two countries. He concluded: 'I would suggest that it is time for this dialogue to begin. Many things could be put right if we were to meet and discuss our differences as equals for the first time in our history.'[5]

There was no specific mention in this article of diplomatic relations, but it naturally gave rise to some speculation, both in the Foreign Office and in the press. George Brown came to the conclusion that, despite many obstacles, including Egypt's continued official adherence to the 'big lie', the time was ripe for him to take a personal initiative to get diplomatic relations with Egypt restored. This was very much his own decision, not based on official advice, and was a departure from normal protocol, which holds that it is for the country that has broken relations to propose their restoration. He relied on the fact that he knew Nasser personally and had got on well with him, and he carried out his decision without reference to the prime minister or the cabinet.[6]

Brown instructed Tesh in Cairo to seek an interview with Heikal and to ask him to transmit the following personal message from Brown to Nasser:

> I feel that I should send you a further message since it seems to me that in the recent difficult months it would have been a great help if we had been able to be in close touch. We have now, I think, reached a point at which, more than ever, a resumption of diplomatic relations between our two governments would make good sense. I need not spell out the reasons: you know how strongly I have always favoured a resumption, and as we approach the end of the second year without diplomatic relations I feel it has gone on quite long enough. I am sure that more contact and discussion between the two Governments at all levels could only be helpful to us both.
>
> I would therefore like to suggest that we might now fix a definite date for the resumption of diplomatic relations between us. The beginning of

October would, I think, be a good time to aim at, and if I knew that you
were agreeable to this I would be very glad for this suggestion to be put
to you in an appropriate formal communication. Could you let me know
what you think about this? If you think it would help, I should be very
glad to send in advance a senior and experienced official, who is known
to you and in whom I know that you have the utmost confidence, to visit
Cairo in order to convey my thoughts to you on the subject.

I look forward to hearing from you and send you my personal good
wishes. Regards. [7]

Tesh was instructed to indicate that the representative Brown
had in mind to visit Cairo if necessary was Sir Harold Beeley.
(Beeley had been ambassador to Egypt from 1961 to 1964 and had
got on well with Nasser.) In speaking to Heikal he was also to say
that Brown had been interested to read his thoughtful article in the
Sunday Times of 10 September. He could allow Heikal to think that
the appearance of this article was an important factor influencing
Brown's decision to send the present message. This message was
delivered by Tesh to Heikal on 14 September 1967.

On 15 September the State Department showed the British
embassy in Washington a telegram from the head of their Interests
Section in Cairo reporting a conversation with Heikal on 12 September. Heikal had commented that it would be easier for the
Egyptian government to restore relations with Britain first (i.e.
before relations with the United States), using Britain's withdrawal
from Aden as a pretext. [8]

On 20 September 1967 Heikal asked Tesh to call and, translating
from an Arabic manuscript, gave him Nasser's reply to the foreign
secretary's message. He welcomed Brown's initiative and would
start working towards the resumption of relations. However, October was too early as he would need to consult the other African
states who had broken relations with Britain at the same time (in
response to the recommendation of the Organization of African
Unity). Heikal added the personal comment that they were ready to

welcome Sir Harold Beeley at any time. They would wait for London to propose a date, but he suggested mid-October.[9] Tesh commented to the Foreign Office that, as well as consulting Arab countries, and perhaps hoping that Sudan would also resume relations with Britain, Egypt might wish to see how things went in the United Nations and in South Arabia.[10]

When this telegram was received, Brown was in New York attending the autumn session of the United Nations General Assembly. The Foreign Office telegraphed its comment to him that the message from Nasser was encouraging and advised him to assume that the Egyptian foreign minister, Mahmoud Riad, to whom it was known that he planned to talk in New York, would probably be aware of Nasser's message, at least in general terms. He could ask Riad to keep the Foreign Office informed of how the consultations were progressing, so that a decision could be made on when it would be best for Beeley to visit Cairo.[11]

In a letter to the Foreign Office dated 26 September 1967, Tesh reported that such mention as there had been in the Egyptian press of Britain's role at the United Nations had been reasonably favourable.[12] Thus one of the two factors that Tesh had thought the Egyptian government might wish to take into account had been safely disposed of. Nor apparently did developments in South Arabia produce any obstacle to progress on diplomatic relations.

Another example of the unofficial channels the Egyptians liked to use was reported by Tesh on 14 October 1967. Claire Hollingworth of the *Daily Telegraph* had told him that she had had a message purporting to come from President Nasser. This was to the effect that he was 'desperately anxious' that the new British ambassador should be Sir Harold Beeley. He did not want to see a 'faceless diplomat' coming from Latin America. The only 'young man' of whom he had heard well was Sir Denis Wright (ambassador to Iran).[13]

This was a most unusual message from Nasser, a fact which perhaps accounted for the very unusual channel through which it had been passed. It is always the prerogative of the sending country to choose whom to send as an ambassador. The receiving country can grant or withhold *agrément*, but it is most unusual for it to ask for a specific person. The ironic thing is that in this case there was no need for Nasser's message. Brown had all along planned to send Beeley to serve for a second time as ambassador to Egypt.[14]

Beeley duly visited Cairo in his 'path-finding' capacity and met Nasser on 21 October 1967. Surprisingly there is no record of his visit in the Foreign Office file. He may perhaps have reported to the foreign secretary orally on his return to London, perhaps in the latter's home, with no-one to make a record of the conversation. However, there was a report from George Brown to his cabinet colleagues covering this subject. In it Brown said that it was agreed at the meeting between Beeley and Nasser that diplomatic relations would be renewed in the first half of December. There had been no attempt to extract concessions in return for this agreement and Nasser had in effect apologized for the 'big lie' about British collusion with Israel in the June 1967 war.[15]

On 31 October 1967 the foreign secretary put before his cabinet colleagues a memorandum on 'Resumption of Diplomatic Relations with the United Arab Republic'. Brown evidently thought this necessary because resumption was controversial in Britain. There had been many angry letters to him from the public criticizing his 'running after' Nasser, some from Jews and some from right-wing anti-Nasser Tories.[16]

Brown argued in his memorandum to the cabinet that the United Arab Republic was and would remain the most influential Arab state. Its attitude would be crucial to a Middle East settlement and to the reopening of the Suez Canal. Iraq and Sudan would probably follow the United Arab Republic in resuming relations, and Algeria might do so.[17] The cabinet duly approved, with no recorded protest from the pro-Israeli members such as Crossman.[18]

The formalities for announcement of the intention to resume relations proceeded reasonably smoothly. As had been planned, simultaneous announcements were made in London and Cairo, with an agreed text, on 19 November 1967. There had been a short hesitation in Cairo on fixing this date because of the tabling by Caradon in the Security Council of what became Resolution 242 (see Chapter 7), which they had said they needed to study, but they were quickly satisfied that this presented no problem. *Agrément* was given for Sir Harold Beeley to be British ambassador and his date of arrival was agreed as 12 December 1967.

The Egyptians were slower to name their candidate for *agrément*, as there had evidently been some infighting in Cairo (reported by Tesh) as to who was to have this post, but eventually the name proposed was that of Ahmed Hassan El-Feki.[19] He was a senior diplomat currently serving as under-secretary in the Ministry of Foreign Affairs. Tesh, who knew him well, reported favourably on him and *agrément* was quickly given.

There was, however, a last-minute problem about the timing of his arrival, as the Egyptian Special Interests Section in London indicated that this might be in January 1968. George Brown, for presentational reasons, disapproved of so long a gap between the arrival dates of the two ambassadors and decided to send a personal message to President Nasser explaining his problem.[20] He mentioned that a further consideration was that the Queen would be away from London from 22 December until the beginning of February. It was therefore desirable that El-Feki should arrive in time to present his credentials before 22 December. This did the trick. Beeley arrived in Cairo on 12 December and El-Feki in London on 13 December. Both were able to present their credentials quickly, so full diplomatic relations were thereby restored.

On 30 January 1968 the head of the North and East African Department of the Foreign Office, Denis Speares, put up a submission entitled 'Resumption of Diplomatic Relations with the U.A.R.', which reviewed the effects of the resumption.[21] In calculating the balance of advantage, Speares cited the following points as favourable:

(a) A 'package deal' had been ratified, under which sequestrated property worth £E11,000,000 would be restored to its owners or compensation paid.

(b) Nasser had told Beeley that four British ships blockaded in the Great Bitter Lake would be released from the Suez Canal. He had added that he was willing to do this 'mainly for Mr. Brown'. (In fact, Nasser was unable to deliver on this promise, because of Israeli objections to a full Egyptian survey of the Canal.)

(c) The tone of the anti-British broadcasts from Cairo Radio had been moderated, although the improvement was not all that might have been hoped for.

(d) The jamming of the BBC Arabic Service in Cairo had been lifted.

(e) The Egyptian authorities had agreed to overflights of their airspace by British military aircraft. This had been useful during the withdrawal from Aden.

(f) Sudan had followed the United Arab Republic lead in resuming diplomatic relations, and Iraq and Algeria were taking steps towards a restoration. In general, the likelihood of anti-British activities in Arab countries had been diminished.

(g) The British Council was reopening its activities in Cairo.

(h) A property section had been reinstated in the Embassy in Cairo.

(i) It had become possible to talk sensibly with the Egyptians about such matters as credit cover for British exports to Egypt and Egyptian indebtedness. This should improve British exports to Egypt and goodwill generally.

(j) It was now possible to hold discussions with the Egyptians on general Middle East problems. This should be helpful in many ways, especially perhaps in the United Nations.

I minuted my agreement that the balance of advantage was favourable, but pointed out that there had in fact been no diminution in

Egyptian-expressed hostility to Britain's policy in the Persian Gulf. For example, Cairo Radio had not moderated the anti-British tone of its broadcasts on Persian Gulf affairs.[22]

Diplomatic relations with the Sudan

Sudan, as was fully expected, was the first of the other Arab states to follow Egypt's lead in moving towards a resumption of diplomatic relations. Its breach had, in fact, been largely token, with ambassadors withdrawn but the remainder of the embassy staffs left in place as Interests Sections. In the case of the United Kingdom, the protecting power was Italy, and the Interests Section was technically part of the Italian embassy, but in practice it acted largely independently.[23] On 2 November 1967 the Sudanese prime minister, Mohamed Ahmed Mahgoub, sent an unofficial message to the head of the British Interests Section, Norman Reddaway, to the effect that the time seemed ripe for a resumption of relations. The message added that President Nasser would like a resumption by Sudan to precede that by Egypt, to ease Egypt's position in the eyes of Iraq and Syria.[24]

However, Mahgoub's course of action, when the United Kingdom's willingness to resume had been made known to him in reply, was not calculated to speed progress. He told the leading Sudanese newspaper, *al-Ayam*, that 'he did not consider that there was anything to prevent a resumption of relations with Britain in view of her line since the aggression and the attitude she had adopted, which was close to the Arab view point. But the Sudanese would take no step without consulting the other Arab countries that had also broken with Britain.'[25]

This consultation process was put in hand, but was bound to take time, especially as it was extended to include the non-Arab African countries that had broken relations in December 1965 over Rhodesia. It became clear eventually that Mahgoub was aiming to gather together a group of countries ready to resume relations with the United Kingdom along with Sudan. His motive was clearly to emphasize the importance of Sudan as a major Arab and African nation, setting an example to others.

There was also a need for time to set up a visit by a prominent Briton to Khartoum, to parallel the 'path-finding' visit that Beeley had paid to Cairo before the announcement of the intention to re-open Anglo-Egyptian relations. It was soon agreed that the person in question would be Malcolm MacDonald, at that time special government representative for Britain in the East African region.[26]

Mahgoub now told the Italian ambassador formally that he would have talks with Malcolm MacDonald and then consult Cairo, Baghdad, Damascus and Algiers. He expected Algiers to be in favour of resuming relations with Britain soon and he would disregard any Syrian opposition.[27]

The meeting between MacDonald and Mahgoub eventually took place on 25 November 1967. It went well, with Mahgoub speaking about a resumption he hoped to see effected in the last week of December or the first week of January 'at the latest'. But he reiterated his intention to consult the Arab and African countries that were out of relations with Britain.[28]

Things then again moved slowly, but on 22 December Mahgoub's son told Reddaway that the consultations had reached a point where it was clear that Algeria, Mauritania and Somalia favoured an early resumption by themselves and Sudan. Iraq hoped for a 'path-finder' visit. Tanzania was not yet ready. There was no mention of Syria.[29]

Time continued to pass, until 10 January 1968, when Muhammad Ahmad Gamal, the permanent under-secretary at the Ministry of Foreign Affairs, gave 25 January as the firm date for an announcement of the resumption. This would follow a meeting in Beirut between Mahgoub and representatives of some of the countries he had been consulting.[30]

Attention then turned to the text of the proposed announcement. Mahgoub wanted it to mention that Algeria, Guinea, Mauritania and Mali were also restoring relations, but the Foreign Office reasonably pointed out that this would be inappropriate since they had not been so informed by these countries. The outcome was a decision on a joint Anglo-Sudanese announcement, paralleled by a five-power announcement issued by Sudan to which the United Kingdom would not be a party. In fact, at the last moment, Algeria opted out of being mentioned. The announcement from Khartoum for the four powers was as follows:

> The following countries, Sudan, Guinea, Mali and the Islamic Republic of Mauritania, had severed their diplomatic relations with the United Kingdom in support of the Arab and African causes.
>
> Now, and after undertaking brotherly consultations and detailed studies on this question, those states decided collectively to resume these relations. They hope that this stand will inspire the United Kingdom to back all the new justifiable causes.
>
> Those states, while resuming their relations collectively as they severed them before, reaffirm their strong solidarity in serving the principles and justifiable causes of their people.

The joint Anglo-Sudanese announcement said merely that diplomatic relations between the United Kingdom and the Sudan were being resumed. It was issued in London and Khartoum, as planned, on 25 January 1968.

Diplomatic relations with Somalia

The Somali Republic is not in the full sense an Arab country but it is a member of the Arab League. It may therefore be worth recording here that diplomatic relations between the United Kingdom and Somalia were resumed (before those with Sudan) on 5 January 1968.[31]

Diplomatic relations with Algeria

There had been contacts between the Algerian government and the British Interests Section in Algiers independently of the Sudanese consultations. The files on this subject have not been opened by the

Public Record Office despite the 30-year rule. I recall, however, that they involved a 'path-finding' visit to Algiers in March 1968 by Sir Richard Beaumont, ex-ambassador to Iraq, then employed in the Foreign Office. Resumption of diplomatic relations took place on 10 April 1968.

Diplomatic relations with Iraq

There had been considerable resentment in the Foreign Office at Iraq's breach of diplomatic relations, particularly at the way in which it was carried out. Diplomatic, consular and British Council staffs had been given only 48 hours to leave the country, no British Interests Section had been permitted to stay behind, and a trade boycott had been imposed. There was therefore no wish in London to be particularly forthcoming to the Iraqis over arrangements for resumption of relations. Iraq had broken; it was for Iraq to propose resumption.

Iraq of course noticed the signs that Egypt was moving towards a resumption of relations and seems to have judged it advisable to follow suit. The 'big lie', which Iraq had given as its reason for the breach, had fairly quickly lost credibility in official circles (see Chapter 4), even if this was not yet publicly admitted in Baghdad.

The first Iraqi move was made in October 1967. The Iraqi acting foreign minister, Ismail Khairallah, mentioned to the Swedish ambassador (Sweden was the protecting power for British interests) on 23 October that Iraqi–UK relations might be re-established 'perhaps within a couple of months'.[32] The next move came in New York, where on 9 November Adnan al-Pachachi, the Iraqi delegate to the United Nations, told Caradon that he was instructed to say that the Iraqi government hoped for an early resumption of relations with Britain.[33] Strangely he amended this message on 11 November 1967, saying that it was not in fact given on instructions but was only 'a personal expression of hopeful expectation'.[34] No doubt he had in reality been instructed to speak on these lines, but without admitting that he had been instructed to do so.

The Swedish ambassador in Baghdad reported by letter received in Stockholm on 28 November that the Iraqi under-secretary for foreign affairs, Kadhim al-Khalaf, had told him that Iraq would follow the 'British/Egyptian initiative' probably fairly soon and allow British staff to return to Baghdad. He suggested that five Iraqi officials then stationed in Brussels to look after the many Iraqi students in Britain might be allowed to move to London without the United Kingdom claiming reciprocity. If so, a larger exchange of staff between Baghdad and London on a reciprocal basis might follow five to six weeks later.[35] The Foreign Office accepted this proposal.

On 22 November Taleb el Shibib, an Iraqi official working in the Arab League office in London, called on Antony Moore, head of the Eastern Department of the Foreign Office. He said that he had been in correspondence with the Iraqi ambassador in Cairo, who had told him that his prime minister would be visiting Cairo at the end of November and would discuss with President Nasser the question of an Iraqi resumption of relations with Britain. Shibib asked whether thereafter an approach by the Iraqi ambassador in Cairo to Sir Harold Beeley, when the latter arrived in Cairo, would be acceptable to the Foreign Office. Moore replied that, speaking personally, he thought it would be perfectly acceptable. Moore's report had been addressed to me, and I confirmed that any channel could be used so long as the communication was authoritative.[36]

On 18 December the Egyptian ambassador, El-Feki, called on George Brown and enquired on behalf of the Iraqi foreign minister whether the British government was ready to resume relations with Iraq and would be willing to send an emissary to Baghdad as it had to Cairo. Brown replied that Cairo was a special case and that for Iraq it would be better for moves on both sides to be reciprocal. Reporting this to Sir Harold Beeley in Cairo, he authorized the latter to let the Egyptian authorities know, if they enquired, that he would be ready to respond to any approaches from the Iraqi ambassador in Cairo.[37]

The next move came when Beeley presented his credentials to Nasser on 21 December 1967. He reported that Nasser had suggested that, if Brown did not wish to send an emissary to Baghdad, he might send a personal message to the Iraqi prime minister or president, perhaps through the Iraqi ambassador in Cairo. Beeley had withheld comment on the idea of a personal message, but had said that he himself was ready to establish contact with the Iraqi ambassador.[38]

On 1 January 1968 the head of the Eastern Department of the Foreign Office recommended that no personal message from the foreign secretary should be sent to Iraq, but that Beeley should be authorized to tell Nasser that the British government was willing to resume relations with Iraq and that he was ready to have preliminary confidential discussions with the Iraqi ambassador on all aspects of the problem. If these discussions reached agreement that a visit by a British emissary to Baghdad would result in an announcement that a simultaneous exchange of ambassadors would take place shortly, such an emissary would be sent as a matter of form.[39] On 25 March 1968 a written answer to a parliamentary question by Mrs McKay revealed that these inter-ambassadorial contacts had taken place and were continuing.[40]

The remainder of the Foreign Office file has not been located in the Public Record Office, but a new British ambassador reached Baghdad on 1 May 1968.

Diplomatic relations with Syria

Syria was the one Arab country that did not restore relations with Britain in 1967–68. They in fact remained broken until 1973. Syria had all along been the most anti-Western of the Arab states and the most reluctant to abandon the charges of Anglo-American collusion with Israel. In the light of this Syrian attitude, and the relatively slight British commercial interests in Syria, the Foreign Office felt no need to take any special steps to encourage the restoration of relations with Damascus. Brown concurred with his officials on this decision.[41]

The outcome of all these negotiations for resumption of diplomatic relations was that by May 1968 Britain had ambassadors in all Arab countries except Syria. This was a considerable improvement on the situation before the June 1967 war, when no diplomatic relations existed with the majority of the Arab states in Africa. It was also in contrast to the American situation: the US friendship with Israel long inhibited restoration of diplomatic relations. The improvement for Britain must be attributed to George Brown's pro-Arab speech at the United Nations and to his proposal to Nasser for a resumption of relations, despite the departure this involved from normal protocol, both steps taken without the knowledge of the cabinet or even the prime minister. It provides notable proof that a proactive foreign secretary can personally alter the course of international relations.

CHAPTER 7

THE BRITISH PROPOSAL
OF SECURITY COUNCIL
RESOLUTION 242(67)

THE JUNE 1967 WAR had fundamentally altered the situation in the Middle East. There was no longer any way, even for the most patriotic Arab, to doubt Israel's overwhelming military superiority over its neighbours. Optimists in the West, and some in the Middle East, hoped that the new realism engendered by this revelation might provide the basis for a fair and final settlement of the Arab–Israeli problem. The immediate question at issue was the future of the territories that Israel had newly occupied and this became the subject of intense speculation and lobbying at the United Nations.

It was a basic principle of the United Nations Charter that no territory should be acquired by force.[1] Israel itself at first accepted this. As early as 5 June 1967 the minister in the Israeli embassy in Washington, Ephraim Evron, had assured Walt Rostow, the national security adviser to President Johnson, that the Israelis did not intend to enlarge their borders as a result of the war.[2] There was, it soon appeared, one exception to this undertaking, namely East Jerusalem, on which Israel rapidly conferred a new legal status. On 27 June the Knesset passed legislation empowering the minister of the interior to apply Israeli law and administration 'in any area of Palestine to be determined by decree' and on 28 June this power was exercised to declare the unification of the whole city of Jerusalem. A new single Jerusalem municipality was created, including not only the old

Israeli and Jordanian sectors of the city, but also Mount Scopus, the Mount of Olives and some local Arab villages.[3]

Jerusalem apart, the Israeli government was willing to withdraw from the newly occupied territories, but only on its own terms. These were, in brief, genuine peace treaties negotiated separately with each of the Arab states concerned: Egypt, Jordan, Lebanon and Syria.[4] This policy received the full support of the United States government. President Johnson, who was personally sympathetic to Israel and not unmindful of Jewish voting strength in United States elections, had no intention of following the course adopted by President Eisenhower in November 1956, of pressing Israel to withdraw without political concessions from the Arabs.[5] On 19 June 1967, in a public speech, he stated clearly that the United States would not press Israel to withdraw in the absence of peace. He then set out five principles which he thought should apply to an Arab–Israeli settlement. These were:

1. the right of every nation in the area to live in peace with its neighbors;

2. assistance to the homeless and justice to the refugees;

3. freedom of legitimate maritime passage;

4. an end to the arms race in the Middle East;

5. respect for the territorial integrity of all states in the region.[6]

With the passage of time, Israel's readiness to make a complete withdrawal began to be more doubtful. In a telegram received by Eban in New York on 19 June (by coincidence the day of Johnson's speech), the Israeli cabinet set out a decision taken on 13 June that Israel would be prepared to withdraw to the international boundaries with Egypt and Syria in return for the recognition of Israel and a lasting peace, plus demilitarization of the Golan Heights.[7] This last point was a significant addition to Evron's message of 5 June. Moreover, there was no longer, it seemed, a firm commitment to withdraw from the West Bank. That was to be a matter for negotiation, and East Jerusalem was no longer in question.[8] Eban and

Ambassador Rafael conveyed this cabinet decision to Dean Rusk and Ambassador Goldberg on 21 June.[9]

American diplomatic efforts in the United Nations strove to follow up the points made in Johnson's speech, but it quickly appeared that no agreement on these lines was possible.[10] The Arabs, with Soviet backing, insisted on full Israeli withdrawal prior to any ending of belligerency, while the Israelis, supported by the United States, demanded direct negotiations with each Arab state and offered withdrawal only on the conclusion of each peace agreement. This division of views between the two superpowers had already been apparent at a meeting between President Johnson and Soviet Premier Aleksei Kosygin at Glassboro College, New Jersey, on 23 and 25 June 1967.[11]

In view of the deadlock in the Security Council, an emergency session of the General Assembly was requested by the Soviet Union on 13 June.[12] (For George Brown's speech at this session, see Chapters 4 and 5 and Appendix E.) On 30 June a Latin American draft resolution called on Israel to 'withdraw all its forces from all the territories of Jordan, Syria and the United Arab Republic occupied by it as a result of the recent conflict'.[13] This was revised to read 'withdraw all its forces from all the territories occupied by it as a result of the recent conflict'. (This revision was probably made in recognition of the fact that the Gaza Strip was not strictly speaking United Arab Republic territory.) The two 'alls' in this draft were unacceptable to the Israelis and therefore to the United States, with the consequence that, when put to the vote on 4 July 1967, it received only 57 votes in favour and 43 against, with 20 abstentions. It was therefore not adopted, having failed to obtain the necessary two-thirds majority.

The session did, however, pass a resolution on 4 July 1967, by 99 votes to none, with 18 abstentions, declaring invalid measures taken by Israel to change the status of Jerusalem and calling on Israel to rescind these measures.[14] The United States delegate was among those abstaining. This and a resolution on humanitarian relief turned out to be the only positive outcomes of the fifth emergency session. In mid-July the session had circulated to it a draft resolution jointly sponsored by the Soviet foreign minister, Andrei Gromyko, and the United States permanent delegate, Arthur Goldberg, but despite this promising dual origin it failed even to come to a vote because of opposition from both the Arabs and Israelis.[15] In some despair at this failure, the emergency session adjourned on 21 July for a lengthy recess. When it reconvened it still made no progress and was eventually wound up on 18 September 1967, the day before the regular autumn session of the General Assembly was due to open.

At the end of August 1967, as was seen in Chapter 5, an Arab summit meeting was convened at Khartoum. The Israelis interpreted the total negativity of its 'Three Noes' as the prelude to preparations for a new war, and this seemed confirmed when Egypt on 21 October 1967 fired on Israeli ships in the Gulf of Suez.[16] The Israeli destroyer *Eilat* was sunk and the Israelis in retaliation blew up two large oil refineries in Suez. The outcome was a Security Council Resolution condemning all violations of the ceasefire.[17]

Discussions in the United Nations resumed on 24 October 1967 in the Security Council. Israeli foreign minister Eban had persuaded the United States permanent delegate that any withdrawal clause should be watered down to 'withdrawal of armed forces from occupied territories', a vaguer phase cutting out the two 'alls' that had been in the Latin American resolution of the preceding June.[18] However, unlike the Israelis, the United States government had in mind no more than some minor adjustment of the Israeli–West Bank armistice line by an exchange of border territories. This was the intention of an agreed United Kingdom–United States minute.

Caradon took the opportunity of the Security Council debate beginning on 25 October 1967 to stress the need for a long-term settlement of the Arab–Israeli conflict.[19] There was by this time general agreement in the Security Council about the elements that would need to be incorporated into a draft resolution that might win acceptance there. These included Israeli withdrawal from occupied territories (the exact formula being a major matter for controversy), peace and secure boundaries, freedom of navigation through the Gulf of Aqaba, and the appointment of a United Nations mediator or facilitator.

Caradon, as a personal initiative, had for some weeks been drafting and redrafting what he hoped might be a suitable resolution and showing his drafts to interested parties.[20] Gideon Rafael reported that Caradon had shown him a draft early in October. He said of it: 'It was a kind of jigsaw puzzle which he had pieced together from bits of the defunct Gromyko–Goldberg formula, seasoned with ingredients of a forgotten Latin American draft and topped with the idea of appointing a special United Nations representative to act as mediator.'[21] The draft was, he said, a non-starter: 'It did not commend itself either to Israel or to other delegations.'

Caradon continued to work on his draft, with increasing success. On 9 November 1967 he said to the Security Council: 'In all the disputes we have dealt with in the Council I cannot remember one in which there was so much common ground.'[22] He was clearly by then becoming optimistic about the acceptability of his drafting efforts. U Thant said of his 9 November speech: 'It was at this point that Lord Caradon of Great Britain made a statement so hopeful and comprehensive in scope that it ... changed the mood of the Council.'[23]

On 7 November 1967 India, Mali and Nigeria had introduced a draft resolution which was acceptable to Egypt, Jordan and other Arab states.[24] It covered the issues of peace, sovereignty of all states in the area, free navigation, and a refugee settlement. On withdrawal it said: 'occupation or acquisition of territory by military conquest is inadmissible under the Charter of the United Nations and consequently Israel's armed forces should withdraw from all the territories occupied as a result of the recent conflict.' The word 'all' was unacceptable to the Israelis, and Eban made the valid point that, in the historical record, it should not be forgotten that the Gaza Strip and the West Bank had themselves been seized by Egypt and Jordan in 1948 by military force.[25]

On the same day, 7 November 1967, the United States had also introduced a draft resolution embodying the principle of an exchange of land for peace. It mirrored the three-power draft in most other respects, such as sovereignty, navigation and refugees, but on withdrawal had a formulation more acceptable to the Israelis, calling for 'the achievement of a state of just and lasting peace in the Middle East embracing withdrawal of armed forces from occupied territories'.[26] The Arabs were unhappy with this wording, as were several Third World countries and the Soviet Union. Caradon, describing both resolutions as flawed, recommended that the Council should allow some time for private discussions before bringing either of them to a vote.[27] The Council accordingly recessed from 9 to 13 November 1967.

Caradon's drafting efforts (in which he had been assisted by his officials, including notably his head of Chancery, Edward Youde) had so far not been cleared with the British foreign secretary. Caradon now sent a telegram to London, saying that there were two resolutions before the Council, for neither of which he advised voting.[28] To avoid this dilemma, he recommended that the United Kingdom should itself table a resolution, which would thereby absolve him from voting for either of its competitors. He did not suggest that this resolution would attract supporters other than the United Kingdom and it was on this rather limited basis that Brown approved Caradon's proposal.[29] After further discussions with the delegations in New York, including the United States delegation, which reacted favourably, Caradon tabled his resolution on 16 November.[30]

The crucial point in his draft was, of course, its wording on withdrawal, on which other resolutions had already failed. Caradon, on the suggestion of Argentina and Brazil, which had Security Council seats,[31] had divided this between preamble and operative text. The preamble contained the phrase 'emphasizing the inadmissibility of the acquisition of territory by war' and the operative text required 'withdrawal of Israeli armed forces from territories occupied in the recent conflict'. The Arabs at first pressed for insertion of 'the' or 'all' before 'territories', but finally accepted the argument, presented by Caradon at a private meeting with them, that the two phrases taken together were clear enough for their purposes.[32] Eban contented himself with the tacit consideration that preambles to resolutions had no binding power and with that thought in mind he made no public objection.[33] His considered view was:

> While Resolution 242 could not be described as an Israeli victory, it certainly corresponded more closely to our basic interests than we could have dared to expect from the United Nations a short time before. At best, the resolution could become the basis for a peace negotiation. At worst, if the Arab governments persisted in their refusal to make peace, there would be international justification for maintaining our position on the cease-fire lines.[34]

On 22 November 1967 the resolution was adopted by 15 votes in favour, i.e. unanimously (a rare event). (For the text, see Appendix F.)

Despite the acquiescence of the Arab delegations in New York to Caradon's text, there were remaining doubts in many parts of the Arab world about the apparent ambiguity involved in the omission of the word 'all' or 'the' before 'territories'. Caradon faced these doubts head-on in an interview which he later gave to a journalist in Beirut.[35] Drawing on his knowledge of Palestine, he contended that the use of either additional word would in fact have been disadvantageous to both Arabs and Israelis:

> I defend the resolution as it stands. What it states, as you know, is first the general principle of the inadmissibility of the acquisition of territory by war. That meant that you can't justify holding on to territory merely because you conquered it. We could have said: well, you go back to the 1967 line. But I know the 1967 line and it is a rotten line. You couldn't have a worse line for a permanent international boundary. It's where the

troops happened to be on a certain night in 1948. It's got no relation to the needs of the situation.

Had we said that you go back to the 1967 line, which would have re-sulted if we had specified a retreat from all the occupied territories, we should have been wrong. In New York, what did we know about Tayyibe and Qalqilya? If we had attempted in New York to draw a new line, we would have been rather vague. So what we stated was the prin-ciple that you couldn't hold territory because you conquered it, therefore there must be a withdrawal to – let's read the words carefully – 'secure and recognized boundaries'. They can only be secure if they are recognized. I think that now people begin to realize what we had in mind, that security doesn't come from arms, it doesn't come from terri-tory, it doesn't come from geography, it doesn't come from one side dominating the other; it can only come from agreement and mutual re-spect and understanding.

The journalist then enquired whether Caradon had in mind mutual concessions, 'that both Israel and the Arabs would rationalize the border by yielding up small parcels of territory'. Caradon replied:

Yes, I'm suggesting that. And when the representatives of the four prin-cipal powers met together at that time in the United Nations after the 1967 resolution, we all agreed that what we had to do was to readjust the line to make it a reasonable line, and that this could be done one way or the other. It's ridiculous that you should have Qalqilya on one side and Tayyibe on the other; they're next door to each other. In some cases the line cut right through the lands of a village, putting some lands into Is-rael and the rest of the lands, as it was then, under Jordanian control. So they're bad lines. We thought that they should be rectified.

This is an interesting, and indeed important, interview. I can attest that it is completely consistent with Foreign Office thinking at the time of Resolution 242: the Foreign Office liked the idea of minor exchanges of territory along the ceasefire line, in order to improve the eventual border. Hence their willingness to exclude from the Resolution the crucial word 'all'.

The lasting importance of the 22 November Resolution

Resolution 242 has ever since remained basic to efforts to achieve peace between Israel and its four Arab neighbours.[36] Gideon Rafael, Israeli ambassador to the United Nations at the time of the Six-Day War, later said of it:

> The resolution was meant to be a set of guide-lines for the establishment of a just and lasting peace between the Arab states and Israel, and to be the master key which would unlock a conflict which had endured for twenty years. It has shown an unexpected resistance to wear and tear in a swiftly changing world situation, enduring even the shock of the Yom Kippur War. Ever since its adoption, Resolution 242 has dominated the diplomatic scene in the Middle East as the only accepted, though differently interpreted, common denominator.[37]

U Thant said of it in 1978: 'This historic resolution ... is still the only basis on which a comprehensive solution of the Middle East problem is believed possible'.[38] It has been supplemented by other documents but has never ceased to underlie the struggle for agreements enshrining the doctrine of 'land for peace'. Avi Shlaim, for instance, writing as late as 1994 on the 'Oslo Accord', said: 'The basis of all the negotiations [at Oslo] was UN Security Council 242 and the principle of exchanging land for peace.'[39]

It might be argued that its time had come and that, if Caradon had not proposed it, someone else would have done, but it is not at all clear that this was so. It is much more likely that the two draft resolutions already tabled would have been brought to the vote and both of them defeated, with the Security Council then adjourning the debate in despair (as had happened in the General Assembly's fifth emergency session). Resolution 242 can therefore rightly be hailed as a major British achievement. It was certainly considered so by George Brown, who said in his speech to the Commons on 24 January 1968:

> Since we last considered the Middle East, in November, the Arab–Israel situation has shown some improvement. This improvement is due in

great measure to what Britain was able to achieve at the Security Council. Last November, the discussions at the United Nations appeared to be totally deadlocked. A number of resolutions had been canvassed, but all were regarded as totally unacceptable by one side or the other. The House will recall that at that stage no compromise seemed possible.

Up to then I thought that we should not get involved in the partisan exchanges that were going on, but I then decided that it would be wrong to stand aside and watch the deadlock deepen, with all the tragic consequences involved. So I then decided to formulate our own balanced resolution. Thanks to the efforts of my right hon. Friend Lord Caradon, and the delegation at New York, this resolution was unanimously adopted by the Security Council on 22nd November. Of course the fact that a resolution was unanimously adopted was a success for the whole Security Council, but we in Britain can rightly take great pride in what happened.[40]

George Brown, as foreign secretary at the time, here claimed much of the credit for the success of Security Council Resolution 242, in which he had played no personal part. As the head of the Foreign Office and therefore responsible for the activities of all its staff, he can in a sense rightly do so. But the credit can more specifically be given to the drafting skills of the United Kingdom Mission in New York and to the diplomacy of Lord Caradon, who had by November 1967 formulated the text of the cunningly worded resolution and won it the acceptance of all delegations in New York with minimum reference to the Foreign Office.[41] However that may be, there can be agreement that the unanimous approval by the Security Council of Resolution 242 amounted to a major British diplomatic triumph and had a lasting political importance.

There is only one criticism to which the Resolution is really open. This is that there was no mention of the Palestinians, except in their refugee capacity. In November 1967 it was assumed by Caradon, and indeed by all other members of the Security Council, that an Israeli withdrawal from the West Bank (including East Jerusalem) and the Gaza Strip would be likely to mean their being handed back to Jordan and Egypt respectively. That was a natural enough assumption at the time, but it was quite rapidly outdated by the growing importance of the Palestine Liberation Organization (PLO) under its chairman, Yasser Arafat.

When at Cairo University, Arafat had been president of the Palestinian Students Federation. He was soon the leader of *Fatah*, which was formed in the 1950s by Palestinians who saw force as the only way of countering the Israelis. At an Arab Summit Meeting on 13 January 1964, the Palestine Liberation Organization was created, with Ahmed Shuqairi as its original chairman. In March 1968 the PLO took part, alongside the Arab Legion, in the battle against the Israelis at Karamah in Jordan and achieved a relative triumph.[42] But Shuqairi was a somewhat ineffectual leader, with whom King Hussein was always at loggerheads. At the Palestine National Congress held in Cairo in February 1969, he stepped aside in favour of Arafat, who became chairman of the PLO Executive Committee. From then on, by a judicious combination of force and diplomacy on Arafat's part, the PLO increased in importance and in international recognition.[43] Its claim to a Palestinian state in the West Bank and the Gaza Strip (and for a long time in the whole of Palestine) was supported by the Arab League and eventually accepted by King Hussein, who at the Arab Summit Meeting in Rabat in October 1974 withdrew any further Jordanian claim to sovereignty over the West Bank.

However, a criticism of Resolution 242 on this ground can be made only from the point of view of hindsight. It does not in the least detract from the importance and validity of the British-drafted Security Council Resolution 242 at the time of its drafting and of its unanimous acceptance by the Security Council. Nor does it really detract from its continuing importance in the search for Middle East peace.

CHAPTER 8

GUNNAR JARRING'S
MISSION IMPOSSIBLE

IT WAS A RARE EVENT. When, on 22 November 1967, a British draft resolution[1] was adopted as Security Council Resolution 242, and that by unanimity, the delegates and their staffs burst into spontaneous applause. Since the end of the Six-Day War on 11 June 1967, there had been over five months of deadlock in the Security Council and the General Assembly. No draft resolution had been able to muster sufficient positive votes for adoption. Even a draft co-sponsored by the United States and the Soviet Union had failed: indeed, both Arabs and Israelis had disliked it enough to ensure that it did not even come to a vote. Thanks to the wording of the British draft and to the intensive diplomatic efforts of Lord Caradon, the deadlock was now over. For the moment, all concerned looked forward to rapid progress towards a peace treaty or treaties and to the withdrawal of Israeli forces from the territories they had occupied during the war.

When the applause had died away, calmer consideration suggested reasons for less than complete optimism. The Security Council as constituted in November 1967 did not contain Israel or any Arab country, so they had not actually voted for the Resolution. And although it was known that the parties to the war had acquiesced in its adoption, it was likely that they had different private interpretations of it. Nor did the resolution prescribe a clear set of steps to terminate the conflict. Rather, it laid down a framework within which the parties could proceed, in simple terms, to an exchange of land for peace. But how much land and what kind of peace? And by what negotiating process were these vital details to be established?

Resolution 242 at least provided a starting-point. Its third paragraph requested the secretary-general:

> to designate a Special Representative to proceed to the Middle East to establish and maintain contacts with the States concerned in order to promote agreement and assist efforts to achieve a peaceful and accepted settlement in accordance with the provisions and principles in this resolution.

This request of course came as no surprise to the secretary-general. The idea had been suggested by President Nasser to U Thant when the latter had visited Cairo in May 1967, before the outbreak of war, and had been mooted for months in General Assembly and Security Council discussions of the conflict. The British foreign secretary, George Brown, for instance, in his speech to the fifth emergency session of the General Assembly on 21 June 1967, had said:

> I believe that the Secretary-General should nominate a representative, whose standing should be unchallenged, to go at once to the area. This representative should have a proper staff and full facilities. He should advise the Secretary-General on the whole conduct of relations arising from the cease-fire and the subsequent keeping of peace on the frontiers. His task would be both to report to the Secretary-General and to play an active part in relations with all the parties in the area itself.[2]

U Thant had therefore already given thought to a special representative. On the advice of his deputy, Ralph Bunche, his choice had fallen on Ambassador Gunnar Jarring, a senior Swedish diplomat who had earlier served as Swedish permanent delegate to the United Nations, including a spell on the Security Council.

Jarring seemed an admirable choice. It was clear that the special representative should be from a nation acceptable to all the parties to the conflict, and Sweden had remained neutral in its attitude to the war. Personally he was not *parti-pris* to either side. Although he had twice served very briefly in Iraq, his expertise was on Central Asia, and he was currently serving as ambassador to the Soviet Union. U Thant had made sure that his choice would be generally acceptable. In his memoirs he states:

> There was no opposition or even reservation to my proposal to appoint Ambassador Gunnar Jarring for that post. Mr. Eban was delighted at my choice, since he had known Mr. Jarring very closely both at the United Nations and at Washington, where the two had been Ambassadors of their respective countries. Arab diplomats were equally happy, since, in their view, Sweden had taken a balanced attitude towards the Middle East problem, and since Jarring himself was highly respected in United Nations circles for his distinguished diplomatic qualities. The Big-Four governments were also enthusiastic about him.[3]

U Thant had consulted the Swedish government about Jarring's availability and had been assured that they would release him from his duties in Moscow. Jarring himself had of course been approached. The secretary-general therefore announced his choice to the Security Council on 23 November 1967, the day after the adoption of Resolution 242.[4]

Jarring had already made his preparations to leave Moscow. He had secured his foreign minister's agreement that he should have leave of absence from, but not give up, his embassy to the Soviet Union, and he left his wife in Moscow when he flew to New York for briefing. It is not clear how long he thought his UN assignment would last, but the retention of his embassy suggests only a fairly brief absence from his Moscow posting – perhaps three to six months, or at most a year. He would surely have been amazed to know at the outset that the assignment would last until 1991, although admittedly he did not work on it full time for the whole of those 24 years.

Jarring's first task was to discuss with U Thant his terms of reference. The UN Secretariat, including its legal staff, produced two versions of these, one designed for possible publication at some

future date and the other intended to remain confidential. The latter
and longer version went in some detail into the differences between
'good offices' and 'mediation' and concluded from the absence of
either of these terms in Resolution 242 that the special representative
could make use of both of these procedures at will. This turned out
to be untrue, as the Egyptians later more than once reminded Jarring
that he was not a mediator. It might perhaps have been better had U
Thant, in appointing him, given him that title, even though it was
not specified in the Resolution.[5]

The UN Secretariat supplied Jarring with a small staff and rather
inadequate telecommunications facilities, which worked well from
his headquarters but not when he was on the move around the
Middle East. He had the use of a small aircraft, on a monthly hiring
basis.

Jarring quickly reached a decision on his *modus operandi*. He
would establish a small headquarters in Cyprus and then visit the
parties in turn. His schedule omitted Syria, which had refused to
accept Resolution 242 and made it known that Jarring would not be
welcome. It also attached little importance to Lebanon, which had
played no real part in the war. The three vital parties were Israel,
Egypt (officially still called the United Arab Republic despite the
secession of Syria from that union) and Jordan. Jarring largely left
the Palestinians out of his considerations. He assumed, as did virtually everyone else, that the West Bank (or a large part of it) would at
some time return to Jordanian sovereignty.

Jarring began his task under a major disadvantage. Over five
months had elapsed between the end of the war and the adoption of
Resolution 242, and during that time the positions of the parties to
the conflict had hardened. Initially the Israelis had not planned to
hold on to the territories they had just occupied (with the exception
that on 18 June 1967 the Israeli cabinet decided to annex East Jerusalem). On 19 June they decided that, against adequate Arab
concessions, their troops would withdraw from the occupied territories to the borders between what had been mandatory Palestine and

Egypt and Syria. That would leave the Gaza Strip, which Egypt had administered but never annexed, in Israeli hands. As for Jordan, there would be withdrawal from the heavily populated areas of the West Bank, but the details of this were left vague.

Abba Eban, the Israeli foreign minister, who had gone to New York for the United Nations discussion of the conflict, was authorized to communicate these decisions to the Americans for onward transmission to the Arabs. On 21 June he so informed the American secretary of state, Dean Rusk, who showed some surprise at the generosity of the Israelis.[6] However, the Egyptians and Syrians were less impressed, demanding that Israeli troops should be withdrawn unconditionally. Israel left its offer on the table but decided not to make it public.

That left room for second thoughts. By mid-July approval was given for the building of Jewish settlements on Syria's Golan Heights. Consideration was given to handing the West Bank to some Palestinian entity (less than a state) rather than returning it to Jordan, but talks with the Palestinians proved unproductive. On 26 July Yigal Allon tabled in cabinet a plan that was to bear his name. It proposed the annexation by Israel of most of the Judean Desert, a substantial area around Jerusalem including the Latrun Salient, and a 10–15-kilometre strip along the River Jordan. The cabinet discussed the plan but took no decision on it; however, it gradually became the main basis for policy. Moshe Dayan, the minister of defence, proposed the establishment of army bases on the mountain ridge running down the middle of the West Bank. On 20 August it was decided that five such bases should be established. By November, when he was appointed, Jarring therefore faced considerable Israeli complications.[7]

The Arabs had also adopted hard positions. As seen in Chapter 5, an Arab Summit Conference was held in Khartoum from 30 August to 1 September 1967. It agreed on:

> joint political and diplomatic action at the international level to the withdrawal of the aggressive Israeli forces from the occupied Arab ter-

ritory after June 5th, within the framework of the basic Arab commitment and conviction which entails non-recognition of Israel, nor
conciliation, nor negotiation with her, but upholding the rights of the
Palestinian people to their land.[8]

This decision became known as the 'Three Noes': no recognition, no
peace and no negotiations, and was the distinctly unpromising
background to Jarring's mission.

Jarring decided that he should conduct his activities under a
cloak of secrecy. He would not, for instance, talk to the press, nor
hold discussions with ambassadors in the Middle East posts he
visited, even ambassadors of the countries with permanent seats on
the Security Council. His talks would be at foreign-minister level for
the most part and he would use his own discretion about communi-
cating the outcome of such talks to a foreign minister on the other
side of the conflict, unless specifically asked to do so. He would, of
course, report by telegram to the secretary-general, but would not
wish the secretary-general to go into any detail in his communications to the Security Council.

This secretive procedure seems to have flowed from an innate
tendency in Jarring. Brian Urquhart, under-secretary-general to U
Thant at the time, said of him:

> He was a veteran diplomat with old-fashioned, and distinctly Swedish,
> virtues. He was a person of the most rigid and controlled integrity, in
> every sense the opposite of self-seeking or ambitious. A formidable
> scholar and linguist, Gunnar did his own thinking and his own work.
> Although he was very open with me, he was reticent and discreet to an
> exceptional degree. Once when he was reported to have said 'No com-
> ment', U Thant observed, 'I'm sure Jarring would never have gone as far
> as that'.[9]

Jarring set out on his first round of visits to Jerusalem, Cairo and
Amman in December 1967. Although he did not himself talk to
ambassadors in those posts, the latter were able to sound out the
foreign ministers concerned about how the talks had gone. They

showed some surprise that Jarring had remained fairly silent during his initial visits, preferring to listen rather than to put forward any views of his own. The conclusion they reached was that he had not at this stage wanted to run the risk of seeming to take sides. On the whole, that was considered as probably very wise on Jarring's part.

U Thant was under an obligation to report to the Security Council on Jarring's progress and he did so as early as 17 January 1968. He told the Council that it would be premature to comment on the substance of Jarring's talks with governments, since discussions were still in progress and had not yet reached a stage at which conclusions could be drawn. He added that the talks had covered not only the major questions featured in Resolution 242, which were of course the hardest to resolve, but also secondary questions such as the release of ships trapped in the Suez Canal, the exchange of prisoners of war, and 'certain measures of a humanitarian character' (presumably refugees). The round of talks would continue, but U Thant commented that both he and Jarring were mindful of the time factor.[10]

Visits by Jarring to Jerusalem, Cairo and Amman continued. Jarring was thus proceeding by the 'shuttle diplomacy' which Henry Kissinger was later to employ so frequently. The British ambassador in Cairo, Sir Harold Beeley, learnt from Salah Gohar of the Egyptian Foreign Ministry[11] that the Egyptians had asked Jarring to enquire how the Israelis defined 'secure frontiers', one of the phrases used in Resolution 242. Jarring reported back to the Egyptians that he had been told that this definition would only be disclosed in direct Israeli–Egyptian negotiations. This was in fact a standard Israeli position. Their objective was peace treaties with each of their Arab neighbours, which they believed could only come about following direct negotiations. Given the Khartoum 'Three Noes', which prohibited negotiations, that attitude of course severely limited the progress that Jarring could make in his soundings of the two sides.

However, according to Gohar, Jarring had on this occasion been willing to depart from his normal policy of silence so far as to put forward his own 'impression'. This was that the Israelis were thinking in terms of withdrawal from the Sinai Peninsula in stages, their conditions being that the Peninsula should be demilitarized and that they should have free passage through the Suez Canal and the Straits of Tiran. They would not hand back the Gaza Strip to Egyptian administration, but would not themselves annex it. They had not disclosed how many Palestinian refugees they would allow to return, but Jarring thought this might depend on the decision reached on the Gaza Strip.

In the same conversation, Jarring had raised a new point. He complained that he was tired and wished to stop flying around the Middle East. He suggested that all the parties should meet in Cyprus 'to work out a solution'. This suggestion had not been accepted by the Egyptians. They said that they regarded Jarring's task as being not to mediate in working out a solution but to find a way to implement Resolution 242. They asked Jarring to enquire whether the Israelis did in fact accept that Resolution and he undertook to put this question to them when he next visited Jerusalem.

This meeting in Cairo had clearly been of great importance. It dealt with two points that were to preoccupy Jarring for months to come. Could he get the parties to come to Cyprus for meetings which he would organize? And did Israel fully accept the provisions of Resolution 242?

This last point was indeed in some doubt. Eban in his memoirs records his attitude as follows:

> While Resolution 242 could not be described as an Israeli victory, it certainly corresponded more closely to our basic interests than we could have dared to expect from the United Nations a short time before. At best, the resolution could become the basis for a peace negotiation. At worst, if the Arab governments persisted in their refusal to make peace,

there would be international justification for maintaining our position on the cease-fire lines.[12]

The Americans probed the Israelis' position at the beginning of February, both in the United Nations corridors and in Washington. They told the British ambassador that they had received evasive replies.[13]

Caradon was also able to inform the Foreign Office on 2 February of information on Jarring which he had learnt from U Thant.[14] He had been told that Jarring was pressing persistently for 'Bunche-type talks', by which was meant talks with the two sides in adjoining rooms with Jarring moving between them. (This had been the procedure used by Ralph Bunche in 1948 to negotiate the armistice agreements, with the two sides only coming together for signature.) Jarring was reported to believe that both sides were agreeable in principle, but the Egyptians were demanding that withdrawal should be dealt with first.

Information also reached the Foreign Office on 2 February from Tel Aviv. Michael Hadow, the British ambassador, had learnt from the Israelis that Jarring was seeking a formula acceptable to both Israel and the Egyptians to permit talks between them. He had threatened the Egyptians that he 'would throw his hand in' unless they showed willingness to talk, and their reply had led him to begin his search for a formula. (This is the first recorded instance of Jarring using a threat to abandon his mission as pressure for progress. It was a tactic that he was to employ on many future occasions, though perhaps never seriously, and with only moderate success.)

On 7 February information about Israel's position reached the Foreign Office from two quarters. The new Israeli ambassador to the United Nations, Yosef Tekoah, called on Caradon and claimed that the Israelis had responded positively to all Jarring's suggestions to them. They had agreed in principle to exchanges of prisoners of war. They had agreed that the ships trapped in the Suez Canal might exit it, provided they did so to the south. They had said that they would be glad if Jarring convened talks and presided over them.

They had expressed willingness to reaffirm that they stood by Resolution 242. However, they feared that among the Arabs the intransigent spirit shown at the Khartoum Summit (the 'Three Noes') still prevailed. Their wish was that the Egyptians should demonstrate privately, if not publicly, that this negative spirit had been abandoned.

On the same day, the Israeli ambassador in London called on the minister of state at the Foreign Office, Goronwy Roberts, and left with him an aide-mémoire. The gist of this document was that the Israelis had assured Jarring, in response to Egyptian points which Jarring had conveyed to them, that they would not object to the invitation to negotiations coming from him rather than from themselves, to which the Egyptians had objected. Moreover they had no objection to Resolution 242 being specifically mentioned as the basis of the negotiations. The Israeli ambassador asked that the British ambassador in Cairo should make it clear that Britain considered these Israeli assurances sufficient to permit the start of negotiations. They feared that the Egyptians wanted the Jarring mission to fail, leaving them free to go back to the Security Council for a new resolution making withdrawal of Israeli troops the first step to be undertaken. Roberts in reply stressed that time was important and that any Israeli formula should be kept simple. He did not promise that Britain would take the action requested, but Sir Harold Beeley was in fact instructed to speak to the Egyptians on the lines proposed.[15]

Jarring visited Jerusalem on 12 February and, as the Egyptians had requested, asked whether Israel accepted Resolution 242. The reply he received was that 'Israel accepts the Security Council's call, in its resolution of 22 November, for the promotion of agreement on the establishment of peace, with secure and recognised boundaries.' This was not really a clear acceptance and, in particular, it was careful to avoid use of the word 'withdrawal'. The Americans thought this formula insufficiently clear and urged the Israelis to improve on it.[16]

Not surprisingly, the Egyptians, whom Jarring visited on 13 February, rejected the Israeli formula. They insisted that Israel must 'respect and implement' Resolution 242 if progress was to be made (and by 'implement' they of course meant withdrawal of troops). However, the Egyptian foreign minister, Mahmoud Riad, made an important step forward when he told Jarring that freedom of navigation 'could be considered an obligation on the part of the UAR'.[17]

On 14 February Jarring went on to Amman. He was assured there that Jordan accepted Resolution 242 'in its entirety' and had done so since the day it was adopted. He was asked to make this clear to the Israelis and to press them for some assurance that would cover the principle of withdrawal, however generally.[18] No such assurance was forthcoming, but the Israelis did say that if Jarring could get representatives of both sides to Cyprus, they would be willing to leave procedure to him. If he thought it best to begin with the two delegations in separate rooms, they would not object. This was a useful concession.

On 19 February Jarring called again on Eban. There had evidently been fresh consideration in the Israeli cabinet of the formula regarding Resolution 242, no doubt in response to American pressure which had gone so far as a letter from Rusk to Eban,[19] and Eban gave Jarring a new formulation. This ran:

> The Government of Israel, out of respect for the Security Council Resolution of 22 November 1967 and responding affirmatively thereto, assure you of its full cooperation in your efforts to achieve an acceptable settlement for the establishment of a just and lasting peace in accordance with your mandate under the resolution.[20]

Eban told Jarring that this was the furthest that the Israeli cabinet would authorize him to go. Jarring undertook to put this new formula to the Egyptians and to urge them to accept it as sufficient to allow them to begin negotiations.

Both the British and the Americans were becoming impatient at the slowness of Jarring's progress and approached U Thant about it.[21] He replied that Jarring was on his last round of preliminary discussions and might soon return to New York to report. On 26 February a United Nations spokesman issued a statement to the effect that U Thant had told Jarring that an exchange of views in New York would be useful. They could consider 'possible next steps and the prospects for entering upon a new stage in the discussions with the parties'.[22] Jarring arrived in New York on 27 February with the intention of staying until 2 March. He had agreed with U Thant that he would meet the ambassadors of France, the Soviet Union, the United Kingdom and the United States.[23] Jarring's meeting with Caradon took place on 29 February. He explained the differences between the attitudes of the two sides, but said he was still hopeful of getting both to Nicosia.[24]

This information inspired a correspondence in London between the Foreign Office and the Ministry of Defence. The Foreign Office urged that a Ministry of Defence medical centre at Nicosia Airport should be made available to Jarring free of charge for talks between the Arabs and Israelis, should he need it for this purpose.[25]

Jarring had worked out a new ploy for bringing the idea of a Cyprus meeting to a head. He had drafted a proposed letter from himself to U Thant to which he hoped to get the agreement of Egypt, Israel and Jordan. His text ran:

> The Governments of Israel and of the United Arab Republic (or Jordan) have both indicated to me that they accept Security Council Resolution 242 (1967) for achieving a peaceful and accepted settlement of the Middle East question and intend to devise arrangements to cooperate with me in my capacity as a Special Representative in the discharge of my task of promoting agreement in achieving such a settlement. In view of the urgency of the situation with a view to expediting efforts to reach a settlement, I have invited the two Governments to meet with me for conferences within the framework of the Security Council Resolution in (place). I have the pleasure to inform you that the two Governments have responded favourably to the invitation.[26]

The unspecified place was expected to be Nicosia. The text combined some of Israel's and Egypt's desiderata in its phraseology and Jarring had hopes of its success.

These hopes were dashed. Jarring first presented his proposed letter to the Egyptians on 9 March and, to his surprise, they reacted badly to it and declared it unacceptable. Jarring picked up his draft and departed, evidently chagrined at the failure of what he had thought a procedural masterpiece.

On 10 March Jarring called on Eban and recounted his talks in Cairo. He showed Eban the draft letter rejected by the Egyptians, saying that he did so 'for information only'. Eban commented that if he had been shown the draft 'officially', Israel could have accepted it entirely.[27] Perhaps slightly mollified by this reaction, but still considering his ploy a failure, Jarring returned to Cyprus.

It is clear from all Jarring's telegraphed reports to U Thant that his meetings were almost invariably with foreign ministers, Abdul Moneim al-Rifai in Amman, Mahmoud Riad in Cairo and Abba Eban in Jerusalem. He had had a brief meeting with President Nasser during his first visit to Cairo, but Nasser thereafter showed no real interest in his progress: his strategy, about which he was quite frank, was to rebuild Egypt's armed forces in preparation for a further round of fighting to regain the Sinai. In Jordan King Hussein followed Jarring's activities closely and sometimes attended at least part of his meetings with Rifai. He was genuinely aiming at peace with Israel, despite the Khartoum 'Three Noes'.

This situation in Jordan led to a rather surprising initiative by the Israeli government. Abba Eban asked Jarring whether he would be willing to transmit a confidential Israeli letter privately to King Hussein.[28] Jarring expressed doubt about this idea but said he would refer it to U Thant. He did so, pointing out that this would mean going behind the backs of the Jordanians with whom he normally dealt. For this and for other reasons, U Thant advised him to reject the proposal and Jarring duly did so.

The Security Council held an inconclusive debate on the Middle East from 21 to 24 March 1968. There was some discussion of the Jarring mission but nothing of importance emerged. On 29 March U Thant circulated an anodyne report on Jarring's progress, stating that he was 'resuming his contacts with the parties'.[29] This report excited Arab displeasure, expressed to Jarring, because it listed Jerusalem as a 'Middle East capital'.

King Hussein visited Cairo and had a discussion with President Nasser about Jarring on 7 April, of which the British ambassador to Jordan, Philip Adams, was given an account on 9 April.[30] He was told that Nasser had said that he had lost hope of a political solution and was resigned to having to fight it out. However, his army would not be ready to fight for about 18 months. Direct talks with the Israelis would cause a revolution in Cairo and he was not willing to accept indirect talks in Cyprus. Hussein had suggested the alternative of meetings in New York, with which Nasser had agreed. Hussein had left his foreign minister behind in Cairo to work with the Egyptians and Jarring on a formula that might also be acceptable to the Israelis.

Jarring visited Cairo on 8–9 April and had talks with Mahmoud Riad and Mahmud Fawzi (ex-foreign minister, now Nasser's special assistant). He also talked there to Rifai. Jarring expressed pessimism about his prospects unless there was a change of attitude on one side or the other. He might have to put in a final report to the Security Council. Riad advised him against this, suggesting that Jarring might go to New York and continue his discussions there. In the light of these talks, Riad and Rifai abandoned their drafting attempts and Rifai returned to Amman.

When Philip Adams saw King Hussein on 10 April, the King told him that he hoped the Jordanians and Egyptians would stick together at least until after the meetings with Jarring that might take place in New York. Thereafter they might part. He was prepared to 'move far and fast', but the Egyptians would want to move more slowly. However, he hoped by that time to have sufficient blessing from Nasser to move at his own pace.

On 21 April U Thant attended a meeting of the International Conference on Human Rights in Tehran and Jarring flew to join him there. He prepared a situation report for the secretary-general, a copy of which is among his private papers. U Thant recorded the event in his memoirs, saying that Jarring 'reported on the progress, or rather the lack of progress, of his efforts'. He went on:

> By that time, Mr. Jarring had made forty visits to Cairo, Amman and Jerusalem without any progress. Israel was still insisting on direct talks and it wanted any indirect talks limited to procedural matters only. The United Arab Republic insisted that Resolution 242 could be implemented without direct negotiations. It proposed that Mr. Jarring prepare a timetable that would commit Israel to withdraw from all occupied territories, in return for peace.

> There was to be no peace, however, for the events of the second half of 1968 thwarted both the Jarring mission and the Council's efforts to give effect to Resolution 242.[31]

That last sentence was of course written after the event. The 'events' that U Thant referred to were recurrent border incidents in the Middle East and the hijacking of aircraft by Palestinian extremists.

Early in May the Jordanians informed Jarring that, in talks with President Nasser and Mahmoud Riad, they had agreed with the Egyptians that both Jordan and Egypt would be willing in principle to open talks with Jarring in New York. They repeated this to the British ambassador in Amman, adding that they did not wish to call for a further meeting of the Security Council.[32] This seems to have made up Jarring's mind about his tactics. He told the Israelis on 8 May that he would return to New York on 15 or 16 May, not to put in a report but merely for consultations. While there, he would conduct separate discussions with the ambassadors of Israel, Jordan and Egypt. He would thus in effect transfer his mission to New York, although he would keep his headquarters in Cyprus. He might even, he said, be able to achieve direct Israel–Jordan talks under his aegis in New York.

On this relatively optimistic note, Jarring proceeded to New York as planned on 15 May, intending to make an oral report to U Thant on arrival and then decide how to advance. There would be one change in his procedures. Whereas he had refused to talk to ambassadors in Amman, Cairo and Tel Aviv (there were no Western embassies in Jerusalem), he was ready to talk in New York not only to the parties to the conflict but also to the permanent representatives of Britain, France, the Soviet Union and the United States.

After several meetings with U Thant, Jarring saw the Egyptian and Israeli permanent representatives on 20 May and called that afternoon on Britain's permanent representative, Lord Caradon. He told him that the Egyptians had suggested his preparing a timetable for the implementation of Resolution 242, but the Israelis had not liked that idea. His plan now was to press the Israelis to disclose what they wanted as 'secure boundaries'. That was important in itself and also because the Israelis had told him that their ideas on the refugee problem would depend on where their secure boundaries were to be. He wondered whether his mandate permitted him to put forward proposals of his own; at least, he could put forward ideas.[33]

Jarring saw Goldberg, the United States permanent representative, the following day and spoke on similar lines. He said that he knew the Israelis were reluctant to disclose their views on secure boundaries for fear that to do so would weaken their leverage for the direct negotiations which were their principal objective. Nevertheless he would continue to press them on this point. He was also looking for some phrase intermediate between 'timetable', which the Israelis disliked because they thought it would begin with withdrawal as the first step, and 'agenda', which the Arabs disliked for fear that it might lead to implementation of some parts of Resolution 242 with the exclusion of others.[34]

Of course, with Jarring in New York, his private papers in Stockholm no longer contain reports by telegram to U Thant as they had done in previous months. Our information on his activities therefore comes mainly from his talks to Caradon and Goldberg, which continued at approximately weekly intervals.

One such meeting took place on 3 June.[35] Jarring told Caradon that he was not discouraged, even though he could point to no improvement in the situation. He would continue his efforts, since to pack up and go home would do more harm than good. He feared that some Arabs had decided that there could be no final settlement until after the 1968 American presidential elections. He would keep up his talks in New York with the parties, trying to narrow their positions on direct negotiations, but was feeling the need for discussions at foreign-minister level, perhaps somewhere other than New York.

Caradon took the opportunity to sound out Jarring on his views on an article in *The Times* by Cecil Hourani suggesting the creation on the West Bank of a Palestinian state. Jarring told him that he had given this suggestion thought but believed there was nothing to be said for it. Such a state could only survive as an Israeli puppet and it would weaken King Hussein's standing, perhaps fatally. He did not think that it would help to solve the refugee problem. Hourani argued that the Palestinian Arabs should have their own voice in the negotiations for a settlement, but it must be remembered that they were already well represented in the Jordanian parliament and government.

On 18 June Jarring told Caradon that at a meeting with the Israeli ambassador on 14 June he had raised the question of the ships trapped in the Suez Canal. Yosef Tekoah had promised to report this enquiry to his government.[36]

At a lunch with press correspondents on 18 June, U Thant said that Jarring would make a report by the end of July. He did not say what kind of report, and Ralph Bunche assured Caradon that it might be nothing more than a short progress report. It became clear subsequently that this promise was not very welcome to Jarring, who would have preferred to keep silent. Jarring, who had had a further three months' extension to his mission approved by the Swedish Foreign Ministry, planned to take a short leave in Sweden, beginning on 20 June, and was thinking of trying to meet foreign ministers there, beginning with Mahmoud Riad.

This intention was rapidly confirmed in Cairo, where it was announced on 24 June that the foreign minister was that day leaving for an official tour of the Scandinavian countries. Eban was also known to be intending to hold a regional meeting of Israeli ambassadors in The Hague, and Jarring had it in mind to meet him there. Moreover Rifai was coming to London for talks with the British government in the second week in July and Jarring planned to meet him there.

Jarring duly met Riad in Stockholm on 25 June. He told him that he was not putting forward any official proposals but was 'thinking aloud'. His thinking was based on the need to make a start on the withdrawal of Israeli forces. He would like to combine this with Egyptian preparations to open the Suez Canal. There might be a recourse to some kind of international supervision while Resolution 242 was implemented in accordance with a definite timetable. This was the first occasion on which Jarring had put forward ideas of his own on matters of substance and it elicited a substantive response.

Riad said that the Egyptians were not insisting on complete Israeli withdrawal before discussing other aspects of the situation. They were quite ready to arrive through Jarring at a plan covering all components of an agreement. Opening of the Suez Canal to Israeli vessels must depend on a solution to the refugee problem. This was a firm Egyptian position. However, the Canal might be opened to cargoes bound for Israel if the Israelis were prepared to withdraw their troops 30 kilometres from the Canal. Egypt would drop their idea of going to the International Court of Justice about the Straits of Tiran question and would permit the stationing at Sharm al-Shaikh of a United Nations unit not subject to withdrawal at Egyptian request. They would also accept United Nations custodianship of the Gaza Strip, which they did not regard as part of

Egypt. They were not prepared at present to enter into direct talks with Israel but did not consider them impossible at some time in the future if Jarring made sufficient progress. They could not enter into a peace treaty but did not rule out some other kind of contractual arrangement.

Jarring must have been delighted at this very forthcoming response to his 'thinking aloud'. He met Eban a few days later and told him what Riad had said. To Jarring's disappointment, Eban made no similar substantive comment but took the attitude that Riad's proposals made no significant difference. The Israelis still wanted to hear Egypt's views at first hand in direct talks and only then would reveal their own ideas. There were some direct contacts with Jordan of a secret nature, the content of which he could not disclose. The meeting concluded with Jarring saying that he would reluctantly have to put in the progress report to which U Thant had committed him. He did not wish this to lead to discussion of his mission in the Security Council, but thought that any such discussion would probably only call on the parties to make greater efforts to reach agreement.[37]

It will be recalled that the Israeli government had failed to recruit Jarring as a channel for private communications to King Hussein. They did not then tell him that they had already developed another channel. Hussein was in the habit of paying fairly frequent unofficial visits to London, for purposes ranging from shopping to dental treatment. Being an anti-Zionist but no anti-Semite, Hussein had a Jewish dentist there, and in his clinic, as early as September 1963, he had met an important Israeli, Dr Yaacov Herzog.[38] Hussein was a realist, who privately accepted that to recover his West Bank territories after the 1967 war he would need an agreement with Israel. In December 1967, therefore, he took part in a secret meeting in London with Herzog, who was director-general of the Israeli Prime Minister's Office, accompanied by Eban.[39] Eban sounded out the King on the possibility of a peace treaty that would restore most of the West Bank to Jordan, but would keep for Israel East Jerusalem and some territory along the Jordan River. Hussein neither accepted nor totally rejected this suggestion, but enquired about compensation for such territorial loss. Eban made no commitment. These exchanges of views were very preliminary, but were the basis on which the Israelis henceforth thought they could at some time build.

This situation was not disclosed to Jarring, since both the Israelis and of course Hussein wished to keep it secret. Another meeting between Eban and Hussein took place in London in late May 1968, at which Eban referred in general terms to the Allon Plan (not yet official government policy) which would retain for Israel the Jordan Valley and the Judean Desert, as well as an area around Jerusalem. Hussein, who must have had considerable reservations about these ideas, did not reject them immediately, but asked for a specific proposal to be put forward, to which he would reply. There, for the moment, the secret contacts rested.[40]

Jarring next paid a short visit to Moscow, without carrying out any ambassadorial functions there. He saw Kosygin on 28 June and Gromyko on 29 June, before returning to Stockholm.

On learning that Jarring would be visiting London in July to meet Rifai, the Foreign Office had decided that it would be desirable for him also to meet the foreign secretary. The meeting took place on 9 July. Jarring said that despite the difficulties he faced, he hoped to be able, with patience and persistence, to enlarge the area of agreement between the parties. He thought that his mission offered the best hope of progress and was ready to carry on for a considerable time. He did not think that either the Arabs or the Russians were now thinking of a Security Council meeting and, barring some new incident, he hoped to avoid discussion in the United Nations until the autumn General Assembly. Then, when foreign ministers were in New York, would be the psychological moment for new developments.

Jarring considered that Egypt was the key to the problem. There was no fundamental frontier problem between Israel and Egypt, unlike the situation on the West Bank. On the other hand, Egypt was less willing than Jordan to engage in direct talks with Israel, and Jordan's willingness to do so depended on Egyptian acquiescence. An early settlement was needed to prevent the Israeli occupation becoming more deeply rooted. But the deep suspicions on both sides prevented him from forcing the pace.

The heart of the problem was that the two sides interpreted Resolution 242 quite differently. The Israelis saw it as a call for negotiations and insisted that those negotiations should conclude in a peace treaty. The Arabs saw it as a directive to be implemented and argued that the Resolution made no mention of a peace treaty, only of an end to belligerency. Jarring's objective was to narrow this difference. The Arabs had moved to the extent of admitting that agreement on implementation would have to be in the form of a package covering all aspects of the problem. Indeed the Egyptians had given him some idea of the practical arrangements they could accept. He now needed a move from the Israelis. Ideally they should accept that the Resolution was a document to be implemented. Failing that, a statement of their idea of secure boundaries, for instance with Egypt, would give him something to work on. He had put this question to them, but so far without response.

The foreign secretary, Michael Stewart, suggested that Britain might try to get the Israelis to be more forthcoming. Jarring welcomed this suggestion, provided it did not appear that he had asked the British to do so. He had been very careful not to seem to be asking outside powers to put pressure on the parties to the conflict.

Jarring said that his plan was to take a few days' real leave and then return to New York. At the end of July he would make an anodyne report to the secretary-general. In August he would go back to the Middle East but he was not prepared to resume continuous commuting there. He would be back in New York when foreign ministers were gathering there for the General Assembly.[41]

When Jarring returned to New York the Israelis sent three questions for him to put to the Egyptians. They were:

1. Is the UAR prepared to establish a state of peace which would sub-
stitute the state of war existing now for 20 years?

2. Would that state of peace be embodied in a binding contractual in-
strument engaging both parties?

3. As a corollary to it, assuming that the UAR and Israel had found
agreed solutions to all the points mentioned in the Resolution of 22 November 1967, what would be the nature of the state of relations between
the UAR and Israel?[42]

Jarring, who had been feeling frustrated by the negative attitude of
the Israelis, hoped that this first initiative on their part might lead on
to some genuine progress. When the Egyptian foreign under-
secretary, Salah Gohar, passed through New York, he gave him the
Israeli questions, but avoided any immediate comments by telling
him that in view of their importance he wished to discuss them
personally with Mahmoud Riad. He did this for fear that the Egyptian government might evade considered replies to the questions by
saying that Gohar had already expressed their views. Jarring's own
reaction to the questions was that the first really amounted to no
more than the reference in Resolution 242 to a just and lasting peace.
In the second, the word 'contractual' might be difficult for the
Egyptians. He did not expect any very precise reply to the third
question.

When putting all this information to Caradon, Jarring added that
his own plans were to take a few days' leave in Sweden and then
move in mid-August to Nicosia, from where he would begin a new
round of talks with foreign ministers. These might perhaps be in
Europe.[43]

Jarring reached Nicosia on 13 August and decided to pay brief
visits to Amman and Cairo. In Cairo, on 17 August, Riad gave him
the Egyptian replies to the Israeli questions. These were:

1. Yes: on the basis of the November Resolution, Egypt was prepared to
liquidate the 20 years' state of war with Israel.

2. There could be two formal declarations to the Security Council, one by Egypt and one by Israel, covering all the principles of the 22 November Resolution, which might then be endorsed by the Security Council.

3. Following an agreed solution, the state of relations between Egypt and Israel would be as laid down in the Security Council Resolution.

Riad also gave Jarring three questions for the Israelis to answer. These were:

1. Was Israel prepared to implement the 22 November Resolution?

2. Would Israel repudiate certain Israeli public statements which had given the impression that Israel had no intention of implementing the Resolution?

3. Was Israel ready to withdraw forces to the position occupied on 4 June 1967?

Jarring went to Jerusalem on 28 August, when Eban gave him his comments on the Egyptian replies. He complained that these were evasive. Since Israel and Egypt disagreed on the interpretation of Resolution 242, they needed specific definitions of what they agreed to. The Egyptians should renounce the declaration of 'no peace' in the Khartoum Resolution. They had also avoided saying what juridical and political relations would obtain after a settlement. Eban also gave Jarring the Israeli replies to Egypt's three questions. These were:

1. The answer was in the statements to the Security Council made by Tekoah on 1 May and by Eban on 29 May, the key phrase being 'we shall steadfastly maintain our pursuit of peaceful settlement of the Middle Eastern conflict'.

2. Israeli policy was contained in their official statements and in their document of 27 December 1967.

3. The 4 June lines were armistice lines, whereas the United Kingdom representative had said in the Security Council that withdrawal must be

to a permanent peace and to secure boundaries. The boundary must be agreed between the two parties.

In addition, Eban gave Jarring two more questions for the Egyptians:

1. What was the Egyptian view on the 1949 procedure (agreements worked out and signed under United Nations auspices, endorsed by the Security Council and registered under Article 102)?

2. Was Israel correct in thinking that Egypt was proposing the Soviet–Japan agreement as a model for an Egyptian–Israeli settlement?

This exchange of questions and replies came to an end on 11 September when Jarring handed to Eban a further Egyptian communication. Unfortunately this was polemical in nature and did not answer the last two Israeli questions. Jarring and Eban agreed that this communication should not be considered as a 'reply', since it did not in fact mention the Israeli questions. But Jarring's personal view was that deadlock had been reached, much to his disappointment.[44]

On 21 August U Thant told Caradon, who had suggested that the time had come for Jarring to put positive proposals to the parties, that under Jarring's direction a comprehensive scheme for dealing with the refugee problem had already been worked out in the Secretariat. (This paper is in Jarring's private papers in Stockholm. It is based on work that had been done by the Secretariat some years before the June 1967 war and is extremely detailed, giving precise estimates for the compensation that might have to be paid to refugees. It assumed that any return of refugees would be to the West Bank rather than to Israel proper, where it would be impossible for refugees' original homes to be restored to them.)

Prior to the General Assembly, the Russians decided to take the initiative. Early in September they put to the Americans a proposal that matters should be taken out of Jarring's hands and that the Arab–Israeli dispute should be settled by an imposed timetable solution. News of this proposal was passed by the Americans to the

Israelis and subsequently leaked by them. The Americans did not favour this idea but kept the question open by asking for clarification on a number of points. The Soviet approach probably inspired President Johnson to issue on 10 September a new statement of American Middle East policy.[45] He stressed that Resolution 242 was not self-executing and called for an exchange of views on the hard issues. He urged the parties to begin talks on matters of substance, saying that how the talking was done was at the outset unimportant.

On 16 September Bunche told Caradon that Jarring would arrive in New York on 23 September. He had been seen by U Thant in Paris and had appeared very dejected. In his view the Arabs had been ready to put forward proposals but the Israelis had refused to budge. Bunche said that when it had last been necessary to extend Jarring's period of leave from his embassy in Moscow, Jarring had asked for his secondment to be extended for only two months, to the end of October. Bunche feared that, if nothing more encouraging emerged by then, Jarring might ask to be relieved of his United Nations mission. However, it was possible that, as a last effort, Jarring might put to the parties a full plan for a settlement which Bunche was convinced he had by now worked out.[46]

U Thant issued his Annual Report on 26 September. In the section on the Middle East he mentioned the adoption of Resolution 242. He paid tribute to the tireless and persistent efforts of Jarring but regretted that these had not brought fulfilment of the promise of the Resolution in any significant degree. However, he noted that all the parties to the dispute wanted Jarring to continue his efforts.[47]

On 27 September, unknown to Jarring, there was another round of secret talks in London between King Hussein and the Israelis. Eban, who was accompanied by Yigal Allon, showed Hussein the Allon Plan for the West Bank, which Hussein not surprisingly rejected. However, the talks continued, with the Israelis being left with the hope that they would eventually prove fruitful.[48]

With foreign ministers gathering in New York for the General Assembly, it was clear to all that a critical time was at hand. Jarring, who had returned there for a possibly final effort, told Caradon on 28 September that he was worried by press reports of a speech by Eban in Paris, in which he had said that he had a plan to announce on the Middle East. The Arabs had told him that they were very ready to press on with indirect contacts with the Israelis during October, but if Eban's plan went outside, or was inconsistent with, Resolution 242, they would be bound to denounce it.

Jarring feared that there were at least four or five schools of thought in or close to the Israeli cabinet, all differing in their views on a settlement: hence Israeli immobility on the subject. His own thinking was that it might perhaps be possible to get the Israelis to agree to a two-stage approach to a final settlement. In the first stage there would have to be an Israeli declaration of acceptance of the whole content of Resolution 242 for implementation, balanced by Arab pledges of non-belligerency and of respect for the territorial integrity and sovereignty of Israel. These pledges should be enough to relieve genuine Israeli anxieties about their security, since they would precede any withdrawal. There would then be a period of years during which confidence would be built up on both sides. During this period, attempts would be made to deal with the harder problems, such as Jerusalem. At the end, the Israelis would get their peace treaty.[49]

The key public event in the General Assembly was the much foreshadowed speech by Eban on 8 October. This was lengthy and obviously very carefully prepared. It said little or nothing that was welcome to the Arabs but did not, as Jarring had earlier feared, contain anything which would really set back the chances of a settlement. It set out nine principles for the achievement of peace, covering:

1. the establishment of peace in treaty form;

2. secure and recognized boundaries;

3. security agreements;

4. an open frontier;

5. freedom of navigation;

6. readmission of some of the new refugees;

7. Jerusalem;

8. recognition of sovereignty;

9. regional cooperation.

Jarring knew that there were one or two principles here that the Arabs were privately ready to concede, such as 5 and 8. But they were certainly not ready to say so publicly, and in fact no Arab speaker in the General Assembly even mentioned the Eban speech. This probably came as no surprise to Eban, who had told Caradon that the audience he was addressing was Israeli and world public opinion rather than the delegates in New York. However, Eban told Jarring that he would be putting a document to him on how the nine principles could be put into effect. In it, he would explain Israel's understanding of the provisions of Resolution 242 and would describe how Israel proposed that they should be fulfilled. Jarring awaited this document with considerable hope that it might provide a real basis for indirect negotiations under his auspices.

On 10 October Jarring had a meeting in New York with the British foreign secretary, Michael Stewart. He told him about the document that Eban had promised him and his hopes that this might lead on to progress. So far, the Egyptians had been more forthcoming with him than the Israelis. They had made public statements about their acceptance of Resolution 242 and had given him their ideas for a timetable. It was now up to the Israelis to make a forward step. He very much hoped that Eban's document would give some indication of what the 'secure boundaries' they sought might be, though he did not expect to receive an actual map.[50]

Jarring's hopes were dashed. Eban gave him the promised document on 16 October and Jarring passed it to the Egyptians. The Egyptians found it unhelpful, especially as it did not even contain the word 'withdrawal', preferring instead to talk about 'the disposition of forces'. Riad submitted a reply to Jarring on 21 October. The Israelis in turn found this useless, since it did not deal with any of the points in Eban's paper. There was thus no opening for the discussion on matters of substance for which Jarring had hoped.

It was now time for a further extension by the Swedish Foreign Ministry of Jarring's leave of absence from his embassy in Moscow. This time, Jarring asked only for an extension of a single month, to 8 December. The clear implication was that he felt that his mission was moving to its end.

On 8 November Jarring met Caradon again. He said that he had many times urged Eban to give him a written message for transmission to the Jordanians. Eban had promised him this but had more than once failed to produce it. Finally he had given him only an oral message, which contained nothing new of substance. It merely reiterated the need for agreement and direct negotiations. Rifai had been extremely angry at this, in Jarring's opinion rightly so. Nevertheless Rifai had told him that he would be ready to resume discussions with him whenever Jarring thought there was something to justify a meeting.

Jarring went on to say that he felt he should continue his mission despite the disappointing lack of real progress during the General Assembly. He had had frequent talks with the parties, but they had led nowhere. He was not prepared to embark on another Middle East shuttle, but was ready to meet foreign ministers, perhaps somewhere in Europe. Or he might go back to his post in Moscow and wait there for evidence that the parties were ready for new talks. At any rate, he had abandoned his earlier intention to end his mission by the end of November.

Jarring added that he had one remaining hope for progress. He had urged Eban to produce an Israeli statement on withdrawal, and Eban had promised to consult his government about this possibility. But he feared that this would not materialize and that Eban would leave New York without any new message from Jerusalem. The risk now was that all the foreign ministers would go home and merely wait. If so, the situation in the Middle East was liable to deteriorate gravely.[51]

This is in fact what happened. There remained an outside chance that, with Johnson standing down, the United States presidential election might bring to power a new president who would be ready to put real pressure on the Israelis to be more forthcoming. But that was a faint hope. In effect Jarring's inability to make progress during the General Assembly meant that his mission had no longer any real chance of success. He was not fully ready to admit it, and did not surrender his United Nations appointment when he at last returned to his embassy in Moscow in April 1969. Indeed he made further efforts from time to time, as the years passed, to get Arab–Israeli negotiations under way. But his only real opportunity had been to make quick progress and that had proved to be impossible.

The reasons for Jarring's failure are clear enough and were basically outside his control. The views of the parties were irreconcilable. The Arabs had their minds set on Israeli withdrawal. The Egyptians were not prepared to enter into direct negotiation, and the Jordanians, despite King Hussein's personal willingness to contemplate it, found it politically impossible to embark upon it on their own. The Israeli government, although much divided about the terms on which they might possibly settle, were united in regarding their current position in the occupied territories as a comfortable one if the Arabs did not yield to their demands for direct talks. The Egyptians did make some forward steps in their talks with Jarring, but never this crucial one. The Israelis made no concessions to Jarring at all, except to assure him that they would like his mission to continue. Eban used his diplomatic expertise to achieve that result without ever discussing substance.

In later years Israeli comments on Jarring sought to put the blame for his failure on him. Gideon Rafael, director-general of the Israeli Foreign Ministry, said:

The timid reluctance of Jarring to press on with his initiative had a decisive influence on the course of events. His reluctance to act decisively
was probably the main cause for the failure of his mission, inaugurating
a decade of diplomatic deadlock instead of initiating a process of negotiation.[52]

That is a cruel condemnation, since it was Israeli obstinacy, together
perhaps with an unhelpful vagueness in his United Nations terms of
reference, that made it impossible for Jarring to take decisive action.
Eban himself gave a rather different explanation:

Jarring ... was a man of scholarly attainments and high integrity whose
greatest virtue may have been his major defect. His mind moved strictly
within the rational limits of European humanism. He assumed that nations, like individuals, guided their actions by reason. He later came to
learn that logic played a very small part in the history of the Middle
East.[53]

This comes near to a confession on Eban's part that his own government, among others, had ruined the chances of a settlement by
acting irrationally.

As we all now know, a settlement between Israel and Egypt came
about through a process unconnected with Jarring. Following the
restoration of some pride to Egypt through its partial success in the
1973 Yom Kippur War, a peace treaty was reached through Anwar
Sadat's startling visit to Jerusalem and the good offices of President
Carter at Camp David. An agreement between Israel and Jordan
followed after Jordan had yielded to the Palestinians responsibility
for the future of the West Bank. But the fate of the West Bank and
the Gaza Strip, along with the Golan Heights, still bedevils Middle
East politics and threaten the peace of the whole region. This remains the apparently insoluble problem which, despite all his patient
efforts, had finally to be abandoned by Ambassador Gunnar Jarring.

CHAPTER 9

CONCLUSION

THE SIX-DAY WAR came as a surprise to all who were studying the Middle East situation at the beginning of May 1967. As Shlaim says: 'Of all the Arab–Israeli wars, the June 1967 war was the only one that neither side wanted. The war resulted from a crisis slide that neither Israel nor her enemies were able to control.'[1] It is therefore to the credit of the British Foreign Office and the foreign secretary, George Brown, that the danger of war was recognized as early as 18 May, when Egypt formally requested the complete withdrawal of UNEF from Egyptian territory.

Brown's instant recognition that this necessitated a complete change in Britain's Middle East policy, from keeping a low profile on the Arab–Israeli conflict to strenuous efforts to prevent the prospective war, was a proof of his proactive approach to foreign affairs and his clear assessment of the likely damage to British interests that such a war could cause.[2] He rapidly persuaded the prime minister that Britain should seek to keep open the Gulf of Aqaba to shipping to and from Elath, by rousing those maritime nations who, like Britain, had declared this to be their policy in 1957, and by threatening the use of force if necessary.

However, the reduced strength of Britain's defence forces made it impossible for Britain to take a unilateral lead in this endeavour, and the cabinet approved only negotiations to assemble an international consortium to undertake the task.[3] The key to so doing was the United States, and that country's still deep involvement in Vietnam made President Johnson, although he liked the British plan, wary of acting without the full consent of Congress. It was clear that this would be a fairly lengthy process and that Israel was not prepared to wait long enough to put it fully to the test. Israel chose war and was rapidly victorious.

As Brown had foreseen, one result of the war was that the Suez Canal was blocked. Because Britain's trade was so dependent on use of the Canal, the economic consequences for the United Kingdom were bound to be severe.[4] Moreover the Arab countries were misled into believing that Britain and the United States had lent air support to Israel during the war, with the consequence that major Arab oil producers banned oil exports to both countries. Strenuous efforts by Britain and others to refute this 'big lie' were finally successful and oil sales to Britain were resumed after the Khartoum Summit in August 1967, but their transport around South Africa added considerably to their cost. This was a major factor leading to the devaluation of sterling later that year.[5] Indeed, the prime minister's political secretary, Marcia Williams, blamed it for the fall of the Labour government at the general election of 1970.[6]

After the war, Britain badly needed to regain its standing in the Arab world. Because of the 'big lie', several Arab countries had broken off diplomatic relations in June 1967. Others, including Egypt, had already been out of relations with the United Kingdom because of its disapproval of British policy towards Rhodesia. There was a need to get them re-opened. Brown had made a big step towards regaining Arab favour by the speech made at the fifth emergency session of the United Nations General Assembly in June 1967, calling for Israeli withdrawal from the territories occupied during the war and warning Israel against the annexation of East Jerusalem. He followed this up by taking a personal initiative to suggest to Nasser, whom he knew, the restoration of diplomatic relations. This succeeded and the remaining Arab countries, other than Syria, followed suit during the first half of 1968. Thus Britain more than recovered from the political damage caused by the 'big lie'.

In November 1967 Britain had a further diplomatic triumph when Lord Caradon's cunningly worded draft, opening the way for the exchange of land for peace, achieved unanimous adoption in Security Council Resolution 242. As Shlaim says of it: 'The resolution was a masterpiece of deliberate British ambiguity.'[7] It has ever since remained the underlying formula for the search for a settlement between Israel and its neighbours. The British role in this success added to the United Kingdom's prestige in the Middle East.

The resolution led to the appointment in November 1967 of Ambassador Gunnar Jarring, a distinguished Swedish diplomat, as the UN secretary-general's special representative in the Middle East. He faced a difficult task, since attitudes on both sides of the conflict had hardened. Israel in particular did little to help him, stressing the need for direct negotiations with the Arab countries and refusing to say unambiguously that it accepted Resolution 242 and would implement it. It would only withdraw its troops to agreed and secure boundaries and would not say in advance where they intended they should be.

Jarring was by nature a cautious operator and proved unwilling to attempt to force the pace by putting forward his own proposals in an effort to bridge the gap between the parties. He insisted that he was not a mediator and that his mandate was only to help the parties to seek agreement. Procedurally he began by instituting a shuttle between regional capitals, then tried and failed to get representatives of the parties to meet him for indirect negotiations in Cyprus. When he moved to New York and opened talks there with the United Nations ambassadors of the parties, he found them unwilling to discuss matters of substance. A move to Europe put him back in touch with foreign ministers, but an exchange between Israel and Egypt of questions and answers soon proved unfruitful.

October 1968 brought the United Nations General Assembly, with foreign ministers in New York. The Israeli foreign minister, Abba Eban, made a major speech to the Assembly, setting out Israel's principles in the search for peace, but this evoked no Arab response. Frustrated, Jarring temporarily abandoned his task in April 1969, when he returned to his post as Swedish ambassador to the Soviet Union.

Britain had throughout this long process been worried by Jarring's lack of progress and his reluctance to take any personal initiatives in exploring matters of substance. While George Brown was foreign secretary, he made several attempts to speed up Jarring's work by appealing to U Thant to get Jarring to put forward personal ideas, but the secretary-general preferred to leave Jarring to advance at his own pace. Britain was inhibited from advancing views of its own by its wish to appear even-handed in the conflict. It attempted to use British Zionists to put pressure on the Israeli government to be more forthcoming, but this and a personal letter from Harold Wilson to Eshkol proved unproductive.

Michael Stewart, who succeeded Brown as foreign secretary, sent Lord Caradon and me to Washington to urge the Johnson administration to put more pressure on Israel, but this proved a hopeless proposal in a presidential election year. Following Brown's resignation as foreign secretary, the scale of Britain's activity in seeking a settlement diminished, and Stewart made little of his speech and consultations during the 1968 General Assembly. Although he accepted a Soviet proposal for bilateral discussions with Britain on steps towards a settlement, ambassadorial links in New York failed to achieve anything, and a Soviet proposal to the United States to work out a four-power plan which could be imposed on the parties to the conflict won opposition from Israel and no support from either America or Britain. Britain in fact agreed with the Israeli argument that only agreements worked out between the parties were likely to prove lasting.[8]

Britain by this time had ceased to have any direct political commitments in the Middle East, other than its responsibilities for the foreign affairs and defence of the sheikhdoms on the Arab shore of the Persian Gulf. It announced that it would withdraw even from these in 1971, under the Labour government's 1968 commitment to remove all forces from 'East of Suez', which the Conservatives, on coming to office in 1970, did not reverse. Britain's remaining interests in the Middle East were economic and commercial, and these could be pursued without undue involvement in the political problems of the area. The events of 1967–68 were thus the last occasion when Britain, thanks mainly to the proactive character of George Brown, took a leading part in Middle East affairs. His efforts were frustrated by the fact that Britain was no longer a great power, but he and his team achieved a greater degree of success than has usually been recognized.

This success derived largely from the strength of the Foreign Office ministerial team of George Brown, George Thomson and Hugh Caradon. Speaking in 1992 about the 1967 war, Eugene Rostow said: 'We had an especially close relationship with the United Kingdom and there we were lucky in having George Brown as foreign secretary and George Thompson [sic] as deputy foreign secretary.'[9] When Michael Stewart took over from George Brown, and George Thomson was succeeded by Goronwy Roberts, that team was somewhat weakened. Caradon, however, remained in office in New York and continued to devote enormous time and energy to the Arab–Israeli conflict in which he was so deeply interested.

Harold Wilson generally collaborated well with his foreign secretary, particularly during the British efforts to avert the 1967 war, and for the most part gave George Brown in particular his head, which he was very willing to take. Notably, Brown made his pro-Arab speech to the fifth emergency session of the General Assembly in June 1967 without clearing it with London, and sent his appeal to Nasser to resume diplomatic relations as a private initiative. He left Britain's standing in the Middle East considerably higher on his resignation than it had been when he took office as foreign secretary.

The causes and conduct of the 1967 war have been treated voluminously in the published record, especially in Israel and the United

States, but hitherto little has been written about the role Britain played. This was partly because Britain's attempt to avert war failed, and governments spend little time publicizing their failures. Indeed, Harold Wilson, as was seen at the end of Chapter 3, made a duplicitous attempt in his memoirs to conceal this British initiative.

Another rather surprising gap in the record is any account of the activities, as UN special representative, of Ambassador Gunnar Jarring. He has published no memoirs of his efforts himself, although he has deposited his papers on them in the Swedish National Archives in Stockholm (*Riksarkivet*). His efforts at the time attracted intense diplomatic interest in Britain and elsewhere, as evidenced by the huge flow of British diplomatic telegram traffic on the subject now open in the Public Record Office, particularly in the year from November 1967 to November 1968. British efforts to stimulate Jarring into more forceful activity failed, largely because of Britain's inability to exercise any decisive influence on the parties to the conflict, especially Israel.

I hope that in both these respects this book makes some contribution towards filling out the record of British history, and above all of British international relations in the concluding phase of Britain's 'moment', as Elizabeth Monroe has called it, in Middle Eastern history.

BRITISH CHIEFS OF STAFF MEETING OF 29 MAY 1967

NEAR EAST CRISIS. FREEDOM OF PASSAGE OF THE GULF OF AQABA

Introduction

It is HM Government's intention (1) to stand by the assurance given to Israel by the main maritime powers in 1957, that they would support and assert freedom of passage of the Strait of Tiran. HM Government is prepared to contribute forces to multi-national military action in order to implement this intention. The military action envisaged is the provision of a small multi-national naval force to escort merchant shipping through the Strait of Tiran and in the Gulf of Aqaba; this force would be supported indirectly and, if necessary, directly by powerful naval and air forces in the Eastern Mediterranean. The force levels envisaged in the operation would be:

a. Multi-national Escort Force

Three escorts

Four mine counter measure vessels (MCMV)

One supporting tanker

b. Supporting Force

United States 6th Fleet

United Kingdom Carrier Task Group

Light and medium bomber, and PR force RAF

Forces from other nations as may be contributed. ...

4. We first state our assumptions about the principles of operation of the escort force and we then examine the forcing of a passage through the Strait of Tiran, considering actions taken by the escort force, and possible response to hostile action against it, including the actions the supporting force might have to take. ...

Escort Operations

Assumptions

6. To reduce the risk to the escort force to a minimum, it would be necessary to take drastic measures. We have, however, assumed that:

a. Risks to the escort force will be accepted and the onus of initiating hostile action will be placed on the UAR.

b. Our measures will, for political reasons, be designed as far as possible to use the minimum force for the task in hand.

c. In our choice of targets for possible retaliatory action, we shall be directed to seek limitation of the conflict, both as to its level and its geographical scope.

7. Nevertheless, it would be essential that the UAR be left in no doubt that attack on the escort force would be met with immediate and effective response. ...

Role of Escort Force

8. We assume that Allied Governments would offer multi-national escort to merchant ships of any nationality and that escort action would be dependent on acceptance by the owners. If escort has been refused, Allied Governments would authorise the escort force commander to give assistance to a ship which was harassed or attacked.

9. The escort would rendezvous with any merchant ship requiring escort, well clear of the Strait of Tiran, so that before entering the channel it would be apparent that she was under escort.

10. Prior to the passage of the first escorted merchantman, the MCMVs could sweep the main channel with ships of the escort force in support. Thereafter, depending on UAR reaction, the channel should be check-swept regularly.

11. A decision would have to be made for the provision of maritime air reconnaissance in support of the probe. Whether this was provided by aircraft operating from Cyprus or from Aden (with recovery to Cyprus) would involve overflying Israel. ...

15. We consider the following possibilities which might result from the mounting of an Allied escort operation:

a. UAR mining and Allied minesweeping operations.

b. Harassment by UAR forces.

c. UAR shore batteries, naval or air forces fire warning shots.

d. UAR shore batteries or naval forces open fire for effect. Escort returns fire.

e. If escort unable to silence the opposition, Allied air strike against UAR shore batteries or naval units.

f. UAR air attack against the escort or merchant ship. Allied air defence measures in the area of the escort operation.

g. UAR air attacks exceed Allied sustained air defence capability in the area. Allied counter-air attacks against UAR offensive airfields insofar as they can be identified.

h. UAR air attack against air bases (probably Akrotiri) and/or Allied fleet in the Mediterranean. Allied air attack to neutralise the UAR Air Force.

i. Soviet involvement.

Mining and Minesweeping

16. The UAR having declared the channel to be mined, an essential countermeasure would be to sweep. Were a ship to be mined, there would be no appropriate local countermeasure except to continue minesweeping and, if possible, to continue with the escort operation.

Harassment

17. The UAR could establish a 'control point' to seaward of the Strait of Tiran through which all ships were required to be cleared before proceeding up the Gulf. They would publicise the existence of this control point through established maritime channels, making it quite clear that any ship which tried to evade this control and

enter the Gulf without their authority would be forcibly stopped, by sinking if necessary. They would deploy Komars to back their threat. The Allies would then immediately be faced with the choice of two alternatives:

a. To call the bluff, with the knowledge that if the UAR were not bluffing, their Komars would have the capability severely to damage, if not immediately sink our escorts.

b. To launch a pre-emptive strike against the Komars to ensure the passage of our ships.

18. The UAR Navy could also harass the escort force by a physical presence in the confined waters of the Strait of Tiran, which is only half a mile wide at the narrowest point. The escort action would be to ignore this and continue the passage even at the risk of collision. UAR surface craft and aircraft could fire warning shots across the bows of the merchant ships and escorts. On our earlier assumptions about the acceptance of risks, this action should be ignored and the passage continued.

Engagement by Shore Batteries

19. If shore batteries opened fire with warning shots, these should be similarly ignored and passage continued. If, however, the shore batteries opened fire for effect, the escort should return the fire immediately, and if possible continue the passage.

20. Retaliation

A coastal battery, whose fire could be augmented by tanks, could inflict significant damage on the merchant ships and escort and would be a difficult target for the escort to silence. It would therefore probably be necessary for the escort to call for air strike to take out the battery; a pre-requisite would be air reconnaissance of the area to permit a pre-planned strike. Prompt retaliation by air attack against the battery would have the advantage that it would demonstrate convincingly the Allied intention to keep open the Strait. The disadvantage would be that, although this would be a local action and the minimum effective countermeasure, it could be represented by the UAR as an important escalation with a view to alienating world opinion.

21. Combat Air Patrol (CAP). If a CAP were provided for the escort by Allied naval aircraft operating from the support force in the Eastern Mediterranean, reaction could be immediate. If, however, support aircraft were on call by the escort, retaliation against the guns would take approximately 40 minutes. A CAP would have the advantages that it would, by evidence of intent, provide a deterrent and would permit immediate retaliation. It has the disadvantages that it is uneconomic to operate, would from the outset involve overflying Israel or Sinai, and might be considered to be provocative. It would, however, once again place the onus of further escalation on the UAR. Keeping the Allied aircraft on call for support would be more economic, would not involve undue delay in retaliation, and would be less provocative.

Attack by UAR Navy

22. The UAR Navy could attack the escort and merchant ship with a superior force, including destroyers, FPBs and submarines either outside the Strait of Tiran or in the Gulf of Aqaba. As mentioned in paragraph 18 the surface to surface missile threat is formidable. The escorts would oppose the attack, but would almost certainly have to call for air support, thus leading to further escalation.

Attack by UAR Air Force

23. The UAR Air Force could attack the escort and merchant ship with medium and light bombers using bombs or possibly stand-off weapons; additionally fighter ground attack aircraft based in the area might be used. The escort would engage within their limited capability. The escort force could not be made self-sufficient in terms of air defence without a CAP and provision of a SAGW ship (DLG). It could be argued that both should be provided. The advantages and disadvantages of a CAP have already been discussed. To include a DLG in the escort force would be contrary to the concept of providing a small probing force, and would be placing a major unit at

disproportionate risk. The only effective countermeasure to a concerted UAR air attack would be:

    a. To provide a CAP for the duration of the passage.

    b. Should this prove insufficient, it would be necessary to mount air attacks against UAR offensive airfields.

Further Action

25. If the UAR were to attack our air bases and/or Allied fleet in the Eastern Mediterranean, this would extend the conflict beyond the context of purely escort operations and could possibly bring in the USSR. We do not therefore consider this further.

MICHAEL PALLISER'S WASHINGTON MINUTE OF 1 JUNE 1967

Prime Minister

A. General

Britain's stock has risen a good deal in Washington because of the Middle East. In part, this results from genuine appreciation of the alacrity of our response and our willingness to plan together – a sort of quasi-revival of the happy spirit of the 'special relationship'. In part, it reflects a rather spurious 'bullishness' in the stock because of special operations in the market – or, to put it more bluntly, a determination, by constant praise for British initiative and British leadership in the crisis, to make sure that we do not run out on them. 'Are you going to behave as tough as you talk?' was the first thing said to me, with military directness, at the Pentagon. There is a certain scepticism in the air – but then they are a bit sceptical about their own involvement too.

B. The Problems

1. The Middle East

There seems much too little political control. The President is committed to his May 23 statement [expressing dismay at the hurried withdrawal of UNEF and declaring the purported closure of the Gulf of Aqaba illegal and potentially disastrous to the cause of peace]. But opinions vary widely on the degree of political support he commands on the Hill and in public opinion generally. There seems no desire, and virtually no acceptance, for the U.S. to play the Middle East peacekeeper alone: equally, there is reluctance for it to be a purely Anglo-American operation. Yet I found no one, White House, State Department or Pentagon, who really believes that more than a few countries will join in a declaration about freedom of passage and that more than two or three will contribute to a naval force. So what then? Kohler (State Department) thinks that Nasser (and Russia) are bound to win a major political and prestige victory unless Israel attacks (when, in his view, she would beat the Arabs). But U.S. policy is directed to preventing this – and therefore to winning a victory for the U.S.S.R. and Nasser. He seemed unclear as to the conclusion to be drawn from this. But it seems to me ... that the logic of the U.S. position could be, before long, either to be less determined in the exercise of restraint on Israel: or, alternatively, (and this is the line that one senses as not unwelcome in the Pentagon) to press Israel to make concessions – such as recognising that no Israeli ships can be allowed through the Tiran Straits but only those of non-belligerents – which Israel will not accept without war: and then to use the war to force sense (and therefore concessions also) out of the Russians and the Arabs. This is certainly not a conscious U.S. policy. But there is a lack of conviction in what is being tried at present that seems likely before long to lead to a search for (or an acceptance of) something more drastic.

UKMIS TEL. NO. 1202 OF 3 JUNE 1967 TO THE FOREIGN OFFICE

Following for Foreign Secretary from Prime Minister.

I will give you a full run-down of my discussions with the President tomorrow morning. But the main points which emerged were as follows:-

Middle East

A. We agreed once again that whatever action is taken must be multilateral. L.B.J. obviously feels this as strongly as we do and is under very strong Congressional pressure on this.

B. The timetable to which the Americans seem to be working envisages that we will allow up to Tuesday or Wednesday to let it be seen that nothing is going to come out of the United Nations: that thereafter we will publish the maritime declaration: and that it may not therefore be until the end of the week that the question of enforcing it will arise. The Americans think that the Israelis can afford to wait militarily at least as long as this if this is acceptable to them politically. But the President takes a more pessimistic view in general than most of his advisers. He is clearly concerned about the risk that the Israelis will go it alone in the next day or two or that, even if they don't, we shall very quickly reach the point at which everything will be seen to turn on whether the subscribers to the international declaration are prepared to put teeth into it.

C. L.B.J.'s anxieties about the timetable are reinforced by his need for more time in which to get Congress into line. He spoke to me at length about his problems on the Hill.

D. On this basis we agreed that contingency military planning should continue to go ahead on an ad referendum basis to both governments: and the Embassy will try to find out from the Americans before Batosik returns to Washington next week what sort of detailed contingency planning the Americans have in mind. They have clearly done more of this than they have disclosed to us so far. The Americans are also anxious to discuss oil contingency planning with us and the arrangements for this, which are already in hand, should clearly go ahead.

2. In general my impression was that the Americans are as yet far from clear in their own minds about their policy, both political and military. L.B.J. is still asking very pertinent questions to which neither Rusk nor Macnamara seemed to have very clear or convincing answers: and the President is clearly worried by this. As a result there is a distinct tendency to try to push us into the lead. The headline in yesterday's Times sums this up admirably, but I hope by constant repetition I made it sufficiently clear to him that we cannot commit ourselves to a merely Anglo-American venture and that if action is to be taken it has got to be on a genuinely and sufficiently international basis.

WHITE HOUSE MEETING
WITH BRITISH OFFICIALS
ON 2 JUNE 1967

Mr. Rusk said that the need to carry Congress with them in any use of force in solving the Middle East problem was uppermost in American minds. The Congress would not accept the use of force unless it was clear that other possibilities had been exhausted and that force was to be multi-national. Once these conditions were fulfilled, Congressional approval should be obtainable in two or three days. This factor dominated the planning timetable. Military planning had had to be delayed because any leakage about it before consultation with Congress would have been disastrous, but the way should be clear for it by the following Wednesday.

On financial planning, Mr. Fowler made a strong plea for use of the existing bank controls. Any setting up of special machinery would lead people to suspect controls were being planned and set off a run on both the reserve currencies. The existing swap arrangements provided a healthy cushion and it would be much easier to extend them if and when a clear need existed rather than on a hypothetical basis.

On oil planning, Mr. Rusk said that the Americans had seen our study and would be making one of their own. The oil companies were also having talks among themselves and would be having a meeting next week, probably in Europe.

Sir Patrick Dean emphasised the need for coordination. It was true that political, military, financial and oil planning could all go on separately up to a point, but there was some stage at which they had to link up and the political aspects were important to all of them. Mr. Rusk said that he had it in mind to form a small select group for comprehensive planning on the American side and suggested that the British side might do the same. The two groups could then keep in touch. But even so it would be best to leave military planning separate for the present.

In discussion on how severe the pressure was on Israel to take action, Mr. Rusk made the point that economic pressure arising from the extent of Israeli mobilisation should not be exaggerated. Financial help would come in from world Jewry; he expected American Jews to raise 100 million dollars to support Israel. The real pressure for early action was political. Here a significant date was the following Monday when the new Israeli Cabinet was to meet the 'Knesset'.

On Israeli military prospects, Sir Burke Trend said that he had the impression that the British assessment was slightly less favourable to Israel than the American assessment, though we were both agreed that in a purely Arab/Israel war, Israel would win. Mr. Rusk said that the American assessment did not seem to him to be very far from ours. The Israelis were talking of defeating the Egyptians in Sinai in a matter of three or four days, but the American assessment was that, even if the Israelis struck first, they would need something like seven to ten days and the conflict would be a bloody one. During this period there would be the danger that the Russians would feel they could not stand by and they would have to do something.

Sir Burke Trend asked how the Americans rated the chances of the declaration by the maritime Powers. Mr. Rusk said that they had only sent out their instructions yesterday and it was too early to assess the response. Probably quite a number of countries would ask for clarification, in which case the Americans would tell them that the wording about 'assertion' of rights did not mean any commitment to military action in the last resort, though equally so far as the Americans were concerned it did not exclude it. With this clarification, he thought that most of those who had spoken up for freedom of navigation in 1957 would sign the declaration, with the likely exception of France. A problem arose from Israeli willingness to sign the declaration. Logically this was difficult to refuse but it might cause quite a lot of other potential signatories to hang back.

Mr. Rusk made a new point about the declaration to the effect that at some point it might be 'injected' into the Security Council's proceedings, perhaps through the Danish Chairman Mr. Tabor. This might be useful if by the following Tuesday or Wednesday it began to appear that the Security Council's proceedings were getting nowhere.

Mr. Rusk also raised the need to study the possible use of channels through the Straits of Tiran other than the Enterprise Channel which ran close to the Egyptian coast. His understanding was that there were two other navigable channels which were probably in Saudi waters. One of them was winding and difficult but one seemed to be reasonably deep.

Mr. Rusk then read a long telegram from Anderson, who had been on a private visit to Beirut and had been invited to Cairo to meet President Nasser. Much of the telegram contained the standard Egyptian line on how the crisis had come about and on Arab rights, but one or two points were worth recording:

(a) Nasser stressed that his control over the Syrians and the Palestinian extremists was far from complete;

(b) He professed himself confident of victory even if the Israelis struck first;

(c) On the Gulf of Aqaba he did not rule out the possibility of some reference to the Hague Group [sic], though only if this did not take too long. (Mr. Rusk found this surprising, since logically Nasser need feel no need for haste since he was in the position of having established physical control over the Straits.)

(d) On the Palestine refugees Nasser attached no importance to compensation as a method of solving the problem. He thought that even if refugees expected compensation they would not in their hearts abandon their claim to return to their home land. He believed as many as a million wanted no other solution except to return.

On discussion of the effect that war in Sinai might have on the force in the Yemen, Mr. McNamara thought that the effect might not be great in purely logistic terms. The Yemen occupation was a small affair and there was not much shooting going on. But if the Israelis defeated the Egyptians in Sinai this would clearly have an effect on the force in the Yemen, though he found it difficult to assess just what it would be.

Mr. Rusk said that the Americans had information that the International Red Cross were on the point of publishing the evidence they held about Egyptian use of poison gas in the Yemen. They understood that a decision on the publication was to have been taken on the previous day, after which the ICRC would send the statement they proposed to publish to the four relevant Powers (presumably Egypt, the two sides in the Yemen and Saudi Arabia). Publication would then follow later that month.

Summing up, Mr. Rusk said that his nightmare was that Israel might start a war and lose and be in danger of being driven into the sea. Mr. McNamara contested this; the nightmare he saw was that Israel might start a war and win, so bringing in the Soviet Union. Sir Patrick Dean agreed that both nightmares underlined the need for further efforts to prevent war breaking out.

APPENDIX E

EXTRACT FROM GEORGE BROWN'S SPEECH OF 21 JUNE 1967 TO THE FIFTH EMERGENCY SESSION OF THE UNITED NATIONS GENERAL ASSEMBLY

13. May I turn to the British position? Before the fighting broke out I said in the British Parliament that, as a permanent member of the Security Council, the U.K. supported efforts to keep the peace everywhere. I made it clear that we, Her Majesty's Government, regarded the United Nations as primarily responsible for peace-keeping. I repeat here what I said there. We have had long-standing ties of friendship with all the Arab States of the Middle East, and also with Israel. If I may speak personally for a moment, I have for a long time felt a very deep concern for those countries. Our friend-ship with them has, I believe, been a great mutual value in the past. It is my desire to see it renewed and strengthened in the future, and I for one will work for that purpose.

14. The attitude of the British Government is clear. We want the area to be at peace. We recognize that peace demands the greatest measure of justice in its political arrangements. And on this founda-tion the progress of its peoples, especially of those whose need is greatest, must be based.

15. I should like, if I may, to set out certain principles which I believe should guide us in striving collectively for a lasting settlement. Clearly such principles must derive from the United Nations Charter. Article 2 of the Charter provides that 'All Members shall refrain in their international relations from the threat or use of force against the territorial integrity or political independence of any State. ...' Here the words 'territorial integrity' have a direct bearing on the question of withdrawal, on which much has been said in previous speeches. I see no two ways about this; and I can state our position very clearly. In my view, it follows from the words in the Charter that war should not lead to territorial aggrandizement.

16. Reports suggest that one particular point may be of special urgency. This concerns Jerusalem. I call upon the State of Israel not to take any steps in relation to Jerusalem which would conflict with its principle. I say very solemnly to the Government of Israel that, if they purport to annex the Old City or legislate for its annexation, they will be taking a step which will isolate them not only from world opinion but will also lose them the support which they have.

17. Having made clear my stand on this issue, I go on to recognize that in all this both the Arabs and Israel have matters to raise which they are entitled to feel must be heard and must be treated with respect. And we in the international community have our legitimate interests which must similarly be respected.

18. Firstly, there are the interests and welfare of the refugees. This very serious problem has been with us for a very long time. The problem has been made more difficult by what has happened in the last few weeks. We have fallen down so badly on this problem in the past that we cannot live with it any more. I shall have something more to say about this in a moment.

19. Secondly, any settlement must recognize the right of all States in the area to exist in true dignity and real freedom, and that must include the ability to earn their living in assured peace. I understood

this to be the view of Mr. Kosygin, and I hope my understanding was correct.

20. Thirdly, there must be respect for the right of free and innocent passage through international waterways for the ships of all nations. There is, too, the immediate, practical problem of getting the Suez Canal cleared. Once this is done, this great international waterway must be reopened as soon as possible. This is of vital importance to very many countries represented in this Assembly.

21. Fourthly – and now I come to a critical point – if the countries of the Middle East are to live together in peace and develop their resources, they must be freed from the pressures which have driven them to waste their resources in an arms race. Obviously, no Government can resist such pressures if its neighbours are not doing the same. The problem imposes responsibilities not only on the Governments in the area but also on the Powers who are at present supplying arms. The latter, therefore – and of course that includes us – should reach an agreement on this as soon as possible. Already new countries are coming into the business of supplying arms to the Middle East. It is imperative that an agreement on arms limitation should be concluded as soon as possible.

22. I come now to the immediate practical things we can and must do. I shall say first, if I may, a word about humanitarian action, and shall then come to broader political action by the United Nations itself.

23. First, we must deal with the problem of displacement. The aftermath of war is always full of tragedy, and we have all been distressed by the suffering caused to those in the areas where fighting has taken place. I do not think anyone expects a final settlement to be reached during this Assembly. Such a final settlement is going to take time. But meantime our most urgent thoughts must be given to the populations which have suffered and are still suffering from the upheaval of war. It is imperative, if feelings are not to be further

inflamed, or a settlement made still more remote, that the Arab communities whose lands have been overrun should be allowed to stay where they are, or to return if they have fled and wish to come back. We cannot allow these people to suffer further, and we cannot allow what has happened to them to result in a further escalation of the already intractable refugee problem. We must express this intention in any resolution we adopt.

24. But this will not be enough. We must in the meantime lose no time at all in bringing relief to those who have been driven out of their homes and who have suffered directly from the fighting. This problem has been tackled energetically by many voluntary relief agencies which are doing magnificent work.

25. The British Government has sent a major contribution to the relief programme administered by the United Nations Relief and Works Agency for Palestine Refugees in the Near East [UNWRA]. By the end of this year, we shall have contributed $100 million, since 1950, to the UNWRA programme – 14 per cent of the total of all governmental contributions. In particular, as a contribution to the present emergency, we are making a special grant to UNWRA of half a million dollars in addition to our normal contribution. We have also produced substantial relief in kind at very short notice, including badly needed blankets and medicines. We have told the Government of Jordan that we will make a grant to them of £500,000, to be spent on agreed rehabilitation and reconstruction work in Jordan.

26. I am not saying all this in order to boast or to say that we are better than anyone else. I am saying these things simply because they are the practical things which can be done now. If any Member of the United Nations has not yet done anything, it can start today.

27. But when we have done all we can to relieve suffering, it is still our main task in this Organization to keep the peace. There cannot be any greater issue for the United Nations. And this brings us to

the main recommendation I want to make. I believe that the Secretary-General should nominate a representative, whose standing should be unchallenged, to go at once to the area. This representative should have a proper staff and full facilities. He should advise the Secretary-General on the whole conduct of relations arising from the cease-fire and the subsequent keeping of the peace on the frontiers. His task would be both to report to the Secretary-General and to play an active part in relations with all the parties in the area itself.

28. The first task of the Secretary-General's representative would be to make recommendations, in consultation with the Chief of Staff, about the work of the United Nations Truce Supervision Organization. May I say here that the whole world community has every reason to feel and to express the sincerest admiration and gratitude for what the present UNTSO team has done under the leadership of General Odd Bull. General Bull has, in circumstances of the greatest danger and difficulty, conducted his operations with outstanding courage and efficiency.

29. It seems clear, however, that General Bull could do with urgent reinforcement of both men and material. I suggest that the Secretary-General should be authorized to recruit and dispatch at once any extra personnel General Bull may need. He will also need better communications, and the Government of Israel should allow him without delay to reoccupy the headquarters from which he was excluded during the fighting around Jerusalem.

30. This operation and its expansion should be conducted under the direction of the new representative to be appointed by the Secretary-General. But this operation deals only with the cease-fire and the arrangements which follow immediately from disengagement. There is the much bigger and more lasting problem of peace-keeping in the area. It is clear that for this a new form of United Nations military presence will be necessary which will give reality to the preservation of peace in an area which may well be troubled for some time to come. One of the most urgent duties of the Secretary-General's

representative should be to advise the United Nations on the form which a future United Nations presence should take. Needless to say, it should be set up in a form which sets out precisely the conditions under which it operates.

31. As I said earlier, the world looks to us now to do more than state principles and long-term objectives. My Government believes that the principles for a settlement which I have set out today will gain increasing acceptance and support. But that will not be enough. What everyone wishes to see, what everyone expects now, what is desperately required, is some immediate, positive, practical action. It is for that reason that we have to set our minds to the problem.

32. Whatever we achieve by way of statement of principles, it is by the action which follows our meeting here that we shall be judged. This is the purpose of the proposals I have made for more effective United Nations action for dealing with distress, for preventing conflict, for laying the foundations of a just settlement. We must now move to meet the desperate need.

33. Seldom has the United Nations faced such a crisis and such a challenge. Its whole future, on which we all depend, could turn on its ability to handle this situation. I speak as one who for all his political life has had faith, first in the League of Nations and subsequently in the United Nations. At this moment I confess to a desperate anxiety about the future. As I speak now in this emergency session, I feel that the future of the Organization in which we have put our trust is in peril. And I am compelled by the strength of my conviction – a conviction which is shared, I believe, by countless people in different countries around the world, a conviction that the longings of the world depend very much on what we now decide.

34. Some of us remember that we have walked this road before. We have seen once before in our lives the collapse of an international organization, the failure of an international ideal. But what is more, as we meet here we cannot forget that even in the last few days news

has come of new dangers on a scale we can scarcely imagine and a new threat to human survival. These dangers and threats give new urgency to all we do here.

35. If we in the United Nations fail now, if we fail to meet this challenge, if we fail to act now, if we fail to take positive and practical action before we disperse, we shall put in peril all those who depend on us.

36. I have tried to suggest the practical ways in which we might start to resolve the issues which face us in the Middle East. But if we fail to take the straightforward actions open to us, we must consider the consequences. I am not the only man in this Assembly – or, as I learned from the news this morning, outside of it – with children and grandchildren, daughters and grand-daughters.

37. If we fail in an area as dangerous as the Middle East, the chances of the world and of our children and grandchildren going up in a mushroom cloud must be enormous.

APPENDIX F

SECURITY COUNCIL RESOLUTION NO. 242 OF 22 NOVEMBER 1967

The Security Council

Expressing its continuing concern with the grave situation in the Middle East,

Emphasizing the inadmissibility of the acquisition of territory by war and the need to work for a just and lasting peace in which every State in the area can live in security,

Emphasizing further that all member States in their acceptance of the Charter of the United Nations have undertaken a commitment to act in accordance with Article 2 of the Charter,

1. Affirms that the fulfilment of Charter principles requires the establishment of a just and lasting peace in the Middle East which should include the application of both the following principles:

(i) withdrawal of Israeli armed forces from territories occupied in the recent conflict;

(ii) termination of all claims or states of belligerency and respect for and acknowledgement of the sovereignty, territorial integrity and political independence of every State in the area and their right to live in peace within secure and recognized boundaries free from threats or acts of force;

2. Affirms further the necessity

(a) for guaranteeing freedom of navigation through international waterways in the area;

(b) for achieving a just settlement of the refugee problem;

(c) for guaranteeing the territorial inviolability and political independence of every State in the area, through measures including the establishment of demilitarized zones;

3. Requests the Secretary-General to designate a Special Representative to proceed to the Middle East to establish and maintain contacts with the States concerned in order to promote agreement and assist efforts to achieve a peaceful and accepted settlement in accordance with the provisions and principles in this resolution;

4. Requests the Secretary-General to report to the Security Council on the progress of the efforts of the Special Representative as soon as possible.

NOTES

Prologue. The Making of Foreign Policy in Britain

[1] William Wallace, *The Foreign Policy Process in Britain* (London, 1975), p vii.

[2] David Vital, *The Making of British Foreign Policy* (London, 1968), pp 10, 113.

[3] *Ibid.*, pp 47, 51.

[4] Not, at that time, 'Overseas' – a common error, committed, among others, by Vital and Wallace.

[5] Quoted from Patrick Gordon Walker, *The Cabinet* (London, 1970), p 117. The sentence continues 'such, for instance, as the imminence of war between Arab states and Israel in June 1967'.

[6] Wallace, *The Foreign Policy Process in Britain*, p 74.

[7] Walker, *The Cabinet.*

[8] Vital, *The Making of British Foreign Policy*, p 55. Ramsay MacDonald did, however, assume the office of foreign secretary along with that of prime minister in 1924, an unusual procedure.

[9] John Dickie, *Inside the Foreign Office* (London, 1992), pp 263–5. See also George Brown, *In My Way* (London, 1970 and 1971), p 144.

[10] *Ibid.*, pp 265–6.

[11] Wallace, *The Foreign Policy Process in Britain*, p 47.

[12] Harold Wilson, *The Chariot of Israel: Britain, America and the State of Israel* (London, 1981), p 332.

[13] Brown, *In My Way*, pp 227–32.

[14] *Ibid.*, p 227.

[15] *Ibid.*, p 229.

[16] *Ibid.*, pp 230–1.

[17] Dickie, *Inside the Foreign Office*, p 96.

[18] Entry in *Who's Who 1993* (London, 1993).

[19] Dickie, *Inside the Foreign Office*, pp 1–4.

[20] John Coles, *Making Foreign Policy: A Certain Idea of Britain* (London, 2000), p 118.

[21] Wallace, *The Foreign Policy Process in Britain*, p 31.

[22] *Ibid.*, p 9.

[23] See Edward Said, *Orientalism* (London, 1978) for a discordant view that the learning of Arabic and the romanticizing of the Middle East by Western observers can be patronizing to the Arabs.

[24] Since Wallace wrote this, the Centre has been closed, as a result of the civil war in Lebanon. But the proportion of Arabists in the Diplomatic Service remains much the same. For the history of the Centre see James Craig, *Shemlan: A History of the Middle East Centre for Arab Studies* (Basingstoke, 1998).

[25] Wallace, *The Foreign Policy Process in Britain*, p 32. See also Reader Bullard, *The Camels Must Go: An Autobiography* (London, 1961), pp 281–2.

[26] *Ibid.*, p 1.

[27] Wilson, *The Chariot of Israel*, p 336.

[28] Wallace, *The Foreign Policy Process in Britain*, p 61.

[29] The author is of course prohibited from speaking about these in detail.

Chapter 1. The Background to Britain's Situation in the Middle East in 1967

[1] Elizabeth Monroe, *Britain's Moment in the Middle East, 1914–1956* (London, 1963, revised 1981). See also Avi Shlaim, *War and Peace in the Middle East* (New York, 1994); Glen Balfour-Paul, 'Britain's informal empire in the Middle East', in Judith M. Brown and Wm. Roger Louis (eds), *The Oxford History of the British Empire, Volume IV. The Twentieth Century* (Oxford, 1999); Michael J. Cohen and Martin Kolinsky, *Demise of the British Empire in the Middle East* (Oxford, 1998); Wm. Roger Louis, *The British Empire in the Middle East, 1945–1951* (New York, 1984).

[2] Albert H. Hourani, *A History of the Arab Peoples* (London, 1991), p 358.

[3] Lord George-Brown's private papers, Bodleian, Ms. Eng. C5015, dated 22 February 1967.

[4] Hourani, *A History of the Arab Peoples*, Chapter 21; Peter Mansfield, *A History of the Middle East* (London, 1992), Chapters 9–11.

[5] Frank Brenchley, *Britain and the Middle East: An Economic History 1945–1987* (London, 1989), Chapter 18.

6   Avi Shlaim, *The Iron Wall: Israel and the Arab World* (New York, 2000), p 7.
7   *Documents on Foreign Policy*, 1st Series, vol. IV, quoted in Christopher Sykes, *Cross Roads to Israel* (London, 1965), p 17.
8   A.J. Sherman, *Mandate Days: British Lives in Palestine 1918–1948* (London, 1997), p 16 (photograph). See also Bernard Wasserstein, *The British in Palestine* (Oxford, 1991), pp 1–2.
9   Thurston Clarke, *By Blood and Fire: The Attack on the King David Hotel* (London, 1981), p 5.
10 Sherman, *Mandate Days*, p 42. See also Wasserstein, *The British in Palestine*, pp 24–5.
11 Ronald Storrs, *Zionism and Palestine* (London, 1940), pp 46–8.
12 Wasserstein, *The British in Palestine*, pp 2–3, footnote 6.
13 *Ibid.*, p 9. See also Eli Kedourie, *England and the Middle East: The Destruction of the Ottoman Empire, 1914–1921* (Hassocks, 1956 and 1978), Chapter 2.
14 Sykes, *Cross Roads to Israel*, p 25.
15 *Ibid.*, p 56.
16 Sherman, *Mandate Days*, pp 42–4.
17 *Ibid.*, pp 55–6.
18 Sykes, *Cross Roads to Israel*, p 60.
19 Zvi Elpeleg, *The Grand Mufti: Haj Amin Al-Hussaini, Founder of the Palestinian National Movement* (London, 1993), pp 7–15.
20 Sykes, *Cross Roads to Israel*, pp 61–2.
21 *Ibid.*, pp 64–5.
22 *Ibid.*, p 66.
23 *Ibid.*, p 73.
24 *Ibid.*, pp 29–30.
25 *Ibid.*, p 75.
26 Sherman, *Mandate Days*, pp 79–80.
27 *Ibid.*, pp 83–4.
28 *Ibid.*, p 88.
29 *Ibid.*, pp 90–2.
30 *Ibid.*
31 A.W. Kayyali, *Palestine: A Modern History* (London, undated), pp 187–227; Hourani, *A History of the Arab Peoples*, p 358.
32 Elpeleg, *The Grand Mufti*, p 49.
33 *Ibid.*, pp 56–63.
34 Cmd. 5479.

[35] Aaron S. Klieman, 'Bureaucratic Politics at Whitehall in the Partitioning of Palestine, 1937', in Uriel Dann (ed), *The Great Powers in the Middle East 1919–1939* (New York, 1988) pp 128–53.

[36] PRO, FO 371/20822/E7272.

[37] Fred J. Khouri, *The Arab–Israel Dilemma* (New York, 1968), p 27.

[38] Morris Beckman, *The Jewish Brigade: An Army with Two Masters 1944–1945* (Staplehurst, 1998), pp 12–13.

[39] *Ibid.*, pp 48–147.

[40] Mansfield, *A History of the Middle East*, p 232.

[41] *Ibid.*

[42] Louis, *The British Empire in the Middle East*, p 388.

[43] *Ibid.*, pp 388–90.

[44] *Ibid.*, pp 397–419.

[45] Clarke, *By Blood and Fire*, p 294.

[46] Interview with Mrs Lloyd Phillips (one of the evacuated wives), 25 November 1999.

[47] Louis, *The British Empire in the Middle East*, p 417.

[48] *Ibid.*

[49] *Ibid.*, pp 443–5.

[50] Brian Urquhart, 'The United Nations in the Middle East: A 50-Year Retrospective', in *Middle East Journal*, vol. 49, no. 4 (Autumn 1995).

[51] Ahron Bregman and Jihan El-Tahri, *The Fifty Years War: Israel and the Arabs* (London, 1998), p 22.

[52] Louis, *The British Empire in the Middle East*, p 487.

[53] Mansfield, *A History of the Middle East*, pp 232–6.

[54] Bregman and El-Tahri, *The Fifty Years War*, pp 27–34.

[55] Shlaim, *The Iron Wall*, p 31. This is a major point of contention among Israeli historians, with the revisionist version, promulgated by Shlaim and Benny Morris, now carrying much conviction.

[56] Mansfield, *A History of the Middle East*, pp 236–7.

[57] Shlaim, *The Iron Wall*, p 266.

[58] Mahmoud Riad, *The Struggle for Peace in the Middle East* (London, 1981), p 4. See also Hourani, *A History of the Arab Peoples*, p 360.

Chapter 2. Nasser's Miscalculations

[1] The fullest analysis of this strange episode is in Richard B. Parker, *The Politics of Miscalculation in the Middle East* (Bloomington, 1993).

[2] For a first-hand account of this episode, see Major-General Indar Jit Rikhye, *The Sinai Blunder* (London, 1980), p 16.

[3] For U Thant's justification of his decision see UN Document A/6730 Add. 3 of 18 May 1967, and his book *View from the U.N.* (Newton Abbot, 1978), p 475.

[4] Harold Wilson, *The Labour Government 1964–1970: A Personal Record* (Tonbridge, 1971), p 395.

[5] Mahmoud Fawzi, *Suez 1956: An Egyptian Perspective* (London, undated), p 102.

[6] Anthony Nutting, *Nasser* (London, 1972), p 410.

[7] Riad, *The Struggle for Peace in the Middle East*, p 23.

Chapter 3. Britain's Attempt to Avert War

[1] Brown, *In My Way*, pp 135–7.

[2] *Ibid.*, p 137.

[3] *Ibid.*

[4] Richard Crossman, *The Diaries of a Cabinet Minister* (London, 1976), vol. 2, p 355.

[5] Golda Meir, *My Life* (London, 1975), p 297. Confirmed by Gerald Kaufman MP in an interview on 1 December 1999, who called him the most pro-Israeli of all postwar prime ministers. Kaufman acted as his daily link with the Israeli embassy during the 1967 war, conveying to Wilson the Israeli ambassador's account of the war's progress.

[6] Crossman, *The Diaries of a Cabinet Minister*, vol. 2, p 358.

[7] Central Zionist Archives S25/6447, quoted by Louis, *The British Empire in the Middle East, 1945–1951*, p 40.

[8] Crossman, *The Diaries of a Cabinet Minister*, vol. 2, p 356.

[9] PRO, CAB 128/42: CC(67), 31st, 32nd and 33rd Conclusions.

[10] Crossman, *The Diaries of a Cabinet Minister*, vol. 2, p 357. There is no mention of these cabinet exchanges in Healey's memoirs, *The Time of My Life* (London, 1989), but he confirmed them generally in an interview with the author on 17 February 2000.

[11] PRO, CC(67), 33rd Conclusions.

[12] Crossman, *The Diaries of a Cabinet Minister*, vol. 2, pp 355–8.

[13] PRO, DEFE 4/218: DP 49/67 (Final).

[14] PRO, CC(67), 33rd Conclusions.

[15] William B. Quandt, *Peace Process: American Diplomacy and the Arab–Israeli Conflict since 1967* (Washington DC, 1993), p 34.

[16] Personal knowledge of the author, who was present. See also PRO, FCO 28/406/28.

[17] Alexei Vassiliev, *Russian Policy in the Middle East: From Messianism to Pragmatism* (Reading, 1993), p 68.

[18]   Bregman and El-Tahri, *The Fifty Years War*, p 82.

[19]   *Ibid.*, p 83.

[20]   Richard B. Parker (ed), *The Six-Day War: A Retrospective* (Gainesville, 1996), p 18.

[21]   Thomson's report is missing from the PRO, FCO 17 file, but he confirmed this account in an interview with the author on 16 November 1999.

[22]   Quandt, *Peace Process*, p 34.

[23]   Eugene V. Rostow, *Peace in the Balance: The Future of American Foreign Policy* (New York, 1972), p 261.

[24]   Lyndon B. Johnson, *The Vantage Point: Perspectives of the Presidency 1963–1969: A Personal Account* (New York, 1971), Chapter 13.

[25]   Quandt, *Peace Process*, p 34.

[26]   Abba Eban, *An Autobiography* (London, 1977), Chapter 13.

[27]   *Ibid.*, p 340.

[28]   *Ibid.*, pp 341–5.

[29]   *Ibid.*, p 345.

[30]   *Ibid.*, p 347.

[31]   *Ibid.*, p 348.

[32]   Writing later in *Personal Witness: Israel Through My Eyes* (New York, 1992), p 182, Eban described this cable as 'an act of momentous irresponsibility' and adds, 'I later learned that the hypochondriac cables reflected a gust of uncertainty that had come over our establishment.'

[33]   Eban, *An Autobiography*, p 348. The text is given by Yitzhak Rabin, *The Rabin Memoirs* (expanded edition, Berkeley, 1979), pp 87–8. It is clear from Parker (ed), *The Six-Day War*, p 142, that the Israelis had intercepted a signal from Hakim Amer ordering the Egyptian army to prepare to attack and had failed to intercept the subsequent countermanding order.

[34]   Eban, *An Autobiography*, p 350.

[35]   *Ibid.*, pp 351–2.

[36]   Shlaim, *The Iron Wall*, p 222.

[37]   H.W. Brands, *The Wages of Globalism: Lyndon Johnson and the Limits of American Power* (New York, 1995), p 187.

[38]   Kathleen Christison, 'US Policy and the Palestinians, 1948–88', in *Journal of Palestine Studies*, vol. XXVII, no. 3 (Spring 1998), p 22.

[39]   Parker (ed), *The Six-Day War*, p 272.

[40]   Eban, *An Autobiography*, pp 355–6.

[41]   *Ibid.*, pp 356–9.

[42]   Quandt, *Peace Process*, p 34.

43 Bregman and El-Tahri, *The Fifty Years War*, p 84.
44 *Ibid.*, p 75.
45 Shlaim, *The Iron Wall*, p 240.
46 Michael Bar-Zohar, *Histoire Secrète de la Guerre d'Israël* (Paris, 1968), pp 137–82.
47 *Ibid.*, p 311.
48 *Ibid.*
49 There is, for example, no mention of the episode in Ian Black and Benny Morris, *Israel's Secret Wars: The Untold Story of Israeli Intelligence* (London, 1991).
50 Parker (ed), *The Six-Day War*, p 210.
51 *Ibid.*, p 141.
52 PRO, C(67)88 of 29 May 1967. PRO, FCO 17/496/1499.
53 U Thant, *View from the U.N.*, p 248.
54 PRO, PREM 13/1906 of May/June 1967.
55 PRO, PREM 13/1906: Palliser's minute of 1 June 1967.
56 HWV/G-6, dated 31 May 1967, headed 'Memorandum for the President'. Copy obtained from the archivist of the LBJ Library in Austin, Texas.
57 PRO, PREM 13/1906: United Kingdom Mission New York telegram No. 1202 of 3 June 1967 to the Foreign Office.
58 Information obtained from the archivist of the LBJ Library in Austin, Texas.
59 PRO, PREM 13/1906: 'Record of a Meeting in the White House on 2 June 1967'.
60 Quoted by Mohammed Hassanein Heikal in *Sphinx and Commissar: The Rise and Fall of Soviet Influence in the Middle East* (London, 1978), pp 177–8.
61 Wilson, *The Labour Government 1964–1970*, p 399.
62 Eban, *An Autobiography*, p 370.
63 Moshe Dayan, *Story of My Life* (London, 1976), p 251.
64 Lt-Gen E.L.M. Burns, *Between Arab and Israeli* (London, 1962), pp 65–8.
65 Dayan, *Story of My Life*, p 277.
66 Avner Cohen, 'Cairo, Dimona and the June War', in *Middle East Journal*, vol. 50, no. 2 (Spring 1996).
67 Avner Cohen, *Israel and the Bomb* (New York, 1998).
68 Johnson, *The Vantage Point*, pp 295–6.
69 Parker (ed), *The Six-Day War*, p 203.
70 *Daily Mail*, 9 April 1970.

[71] Wilson, *The Labour Government 1964–1970*, pp 401–2.

Chapter 4. The 'Big Lie'

[1] House of Commons Hansard, 5 June 1967, Cols. 629–70 and 6 June 1967, Cols. 797–8.

[2] Peter Paterson, *Tired and Emotional: The Life of Lord George-Brown* (London, 1993), p 220.

[3] PRO, PREM 13/858: Foreign Office telegram No. 469 of 21 May 1967 to Tel Aviv.

[4] Riad, *The Struggle for Peace in the Middle East*, p 24.

[5] Hussein of Jordan, *My 'War' With Israel* (translated from the French) (London, 1969), p 66.

[6] Nasser telephoned King Hussein to coordinate broadcasting of the story by Jordanian as well as Egyptian Radio. See Randolph S. Churchill and Winston S. Churchill, *The Six Day War* (London, 1967), p 90, for the full text of the conversation as monitored in Israel.

[7] Churchill and Churchill, *The Six Day War*, p 82.

[8] *Ibid.*, p 82.

[9] *Ibid.*

[10] *Ibid.*, pp 88–9.

[11] BBC Monitoring Service, Second Series, ME/2484/A/18, 7 June 1967.

[12] BBC Monitoring Service, Second Series, ME/2484/A/23, 7 June 1967.

[13] Paul Gore-Booth, *With Great Truth and Respect* (London, 1974), pp 366–7.

[14] House of Commons Hansard, 6 June 1967, Cols. 797–8.

[15] SCOR, 1348th meeting of 6 June 1967.

[16] *Ibid.*

[17] BBC Monitoring Service, Second Series, ME/2485/A/6, 6 June 1967.

[18] Johnson, *The Vantage Point*, p 287.

[19] GAOR, 1529th Plenary Meeting, 21 June 1967.

[20] Public statement by King Hussein in London, 3 July 1967.

[21] *Look*, 4 March 1968.

[22] PRO, FCO 17/36/34: Tripoli telegram No. 886 of 8 September 1967 to the Foreign Office.

[23] House of Commons Hansard, 7 June 1967, Cols. 1066–8.

[24] Interview with Sir Richard Beaumont, London, 13 August 1998.

[25] Kenneth O. Morgan, *Callaghan: A Life* (Oxford, 1997), p 263.

[26] PRO, FCO 17/36/37: Despatch by Norman Reddaway to the Foreign Secretary.

[27] Brenchley, *Britain and the Middle East: An Economic History 1945–1987*, pp 182–4.
[28] Wilson, *The Labour Government 1964–1970*, p 400.
[29] PRO, PREM 13/1906.

Chapter 5. Postwar Policies

[1] For the preceding paragraphs, see Shlaim, *The Iron Wall*, pp 253–4.
[2] Personal knowledge of the author.
[3] All the foregoing derives from the personal knowledge of the author. Surprisingly, Brown makes no mention of this important speech in his memoirs, *In My Way.*
[4] PRO, FCO 17/493/1297: UKMIS New York telegram No. 1260 to the Foreign Office.
[5] PRO, FCO 17/498: Visit of the Foreign Secretary to the United States.
[6] Crossman, *The Diaries of a Cabinet Minister*, vol. 2, pp 392–3.
[7] House of Commons Hansard, 26 June 1967, Cols. 91–2.
[8] House of Commons Hansard, 31 October 1967, Col. 397.
[9] See Chapter 6.
[10] PRO, FCO 17/36/3: Cairo telegram No. 858 of 28 August 1967 to the Foreign Office.
[11] PRO, FCO 17/36/9: Khartoum telegram No. 486 of 31 August 1967 to the Foreign Office.
[12] PRO, FCO 17/36/12: Khartoum telegram No. 493 of 2 September 1967 to the Foreign Office.
[13] PRO, FCO 17/36/14: Khartoum telegram No. 495 of 2 September 1967 to the Foreign Office.
[14] PRO, FCO 17/36/24: Khartoum telegram No. 505 of 4 September 1967 to the Foreign Office.
[15] PRO, FCO 17/36/34: Tripoli telegram No. 886 to the Foreign Office.
[16] Personal knowledge of the author.

Chapter 6. Diplomatic Relations with Arab Countries

[1] Personal knowledge of the author.
[2] PRO, FCO 39/265/1: Cairo telegram No. 260 of 11 April 1967 to the Foreign Office.
[3] Brown, *In My Way*, pp 137–8.
[4] *Ibid.*
[5] PRO, FCO 39/265/53: Foreign Office telegram No. 1221 of 11 September 1967 to Cairo.
[6] Personal knowledge of author.

[7]   PRO, FCO 39/266/6: Foreign Office telegram No. 1229 of 12 September 1967 to Cairo.

[8]   PRO, FCO 39/266/78: Washington telegram No. 2972 of 15 September 1967 to the Foreign Office.

[9]   PRO, FCO 39/266/101: Cairo telegram No. 934 of 21 September 1967 to the Foreign Office.

[10] PRO, FCO 39/266/102: Cairo telegram No. 938 of 21 September 1967 to the Foreign Office.

[11] PRO, FCO 39/266/105: Foreign Office telegram No. 5066 of 22 September 1967 to UKMIS New York.

[12] PRO, FCO 39/267/113A: Letter from Tesh to the Foreign Office of 26 September 1967.

[13] PRO, FCO 39/267/148: Cairo telegram No. 1021 of 14 October 1967 to the Foreign Office.

[14] Personal knowledge of the author.

[15] PRO, FCO 39/267/163.

[16] Personal knowledge of the author.

[17] PRO, C(67)172, 31 October 1967.

[18] PRO, C.C.(67): 63rd meeting on 2 November 1967.

[19] PRO, FCO 39/269/266.

[20] FCO telegram No. 1853 of 5 December 1967 to Cairo (draft only in PRO file).

[21] PRO, FCO 39/269/285.

[22] *Ibid.*

[23] Personal knowledge of the author.

[24] PRO, FCO 39/191/104: Khartoum telegram No. 623 of 2 November 1967 to the Foreign Office.

[25] PRO, FCO 39/191/114: Khartoum telegram No. 627 of 6 November 1967 to the Foreign Office.

[26] PRO, FCO 39/191/118: Khartoum telegram No. 631 of 7 November 1967 to the Foreign Office.

[27] PRO, FCO 39/191/143: Khartoum telegram No. 666 of 21 November 1967 to the Foreign Office.

[28] PRO, FCO 39/192/149: Khartoum telegram No. 674 of 25 November 1967 to the Foreign Office.

[29] PRO, FCO 39/192/172: Khartoum telegram No. 723 of 23 December 1967 to the Foreign Office.

[30] PRO, FCO 39/192/177: Khartoum telegram No. 12 of 10 January 1968 to the Foreign Office.

[31] PRO, FCO 39/170/1.

[32] PRO, FCO 17/434/64: Stockholm telegram No. 565 of 26 October 1967 to the Foreign Office.

[33] PRO, FCO 17/434/unnumbered: UKMIS New York telegram No. 3124 of 9 November 1967 to the Foreign Office.

[34] PRO, FCO 17/434/67: UKMIS New York telegram No. 3162 of 11 November 1967 to the Foreign Office.

[35] PRO, FCO 17/434/69: Stockholm telegram No. 648 of 28 November 1967 to the Foreign Office.

[36] PRO, FCO 17/434/75.

[37] PRO, FCO/17/434/78: Foreign Office telegram No. 1950 of 19 December 1967 to Cairo.

[38] PRO, FCO/17/434/unnumbered: Cairo telegram No. 1306 of 22 December 1967 to the Foreign Office.

[39] PRO, FCO/17/434/83, 1 January 1968.

[40] House of Commons Hansard, 25 March 1968, Cols. 194–5.

[41] Personal knowledge of the author.

Chapter 7. The British Proposal of Security Council Resolution 242(67)

[1] United Nations Charter, Chapter 2.

[2] Quandt, *Peace Process*, p 54.

[3] Mark Tessler, *A History of the Israeli–Palestinian Conflict* (Bloomington, 1994), pp 403–4.

[4] Eban, *An Autobiography*, p 434 and p 436.

[5] Quandt, *Peace Process*, p 54.

[6] *Public Papers of the Presidents of the United States: Lyndon B. Johnson, 1967*, Part I, pp 632–4.

[7] Bregman and El-Tahri, *The Fifty Years War*, pp 99–100.

[8] Quandt, *Peace Process*, p 52.

[9] Bregman and El-Tahri, *The Fifty Years War*, pp 99–100.

[10] Quandt, *Peace Process*, p 55.

[11] Tessler, *A History of the Israeli–Palestinian Conflict*, p 407.

[12] UN Document A/6717, 13 June 1967.

[13] UN Document A/L.523, 30 June 1967.

[14] Resolution 2253 (ES-V), 4 July 1967.

[15] Tessler, *A History of the Israeli–Palestinian Conflict*, p 408.

[16] *Ibid.*, p 409.

[17] UN Document S/8213.

[18] Eban, *An Autobiography*, p 450.

[19] SCOR, 1373rd meeting of 9/10 November 1967, paragraph 168.

[20] Tessler, *A History of the Israeli–Palestinian Conflict*, p 415.

[21] Gideon Rafael, *Destination Peace: Three Decades of Israeli Foreign Policy: A Personal Memoir* (London, 1981), p 185.

[22] SCOR, 1373rd meeting of 9/10 November 1967, para.168.

[23] U Thant, *View from the U.N.*, p 292.

[24] S/8227, 7 November 1967.

[25] SCOR, 1375th meeting of 13 November 1967, paragraph 48.

[26] S/8229, 7 November 1967.

[27] SCOR, 1373rd meeting of 9 November 1967, paragraph 182.

[28] UKMIS New York telegram to the Foreign Office (missing from the PRO file).

[29] Foreign Office telegram to UKMIS New York (missing from the PRO file).

[30] UN Document S/8247, 16 November 1967.

[31] Rafael, *Destination Peace*, pp 187–8.

[32] Riad, *The Struggle for Peace in the Middle East*, p 69.

[33] Eban, *An Autobiography*, p 453.

[34] *Ibid.*

[35] Hisham Sharabi, 'An Interview with Lord Caradon', in *Journal of Palestine Studies*, vol. V, (1976), pp 142–52.

[36] Shlaim, *War and Peace in the Middle East*, p 44.

[37] Rafael, *Destination Peace*, p 190.

[38] U Thant, *View from the U.N.*, p 293.

[39] Avi Shlaim, 'The Oslo Accord', in *Journal of Palestine Studies*, vol. XXIII, no. 3 (1994), p 27.

[40] House of Commons Hansard, 24 January 1968, Cols. 440–1.

[41] Personal knowledge of the author.

[42] The Israelis attacked Karamah, a *Fatah* base in a refugee camp on the east side of the Jordan River, as a reprisal for a guerrilla raid on Israel. It was more strongly defended than they had expected and there were quite heavy casualties on both sides, including Jordanian civilians. See General Odd Bull, *War and Peace in the Middle East: The Experiences and Views of a U.N. Observer* (London, 1976), pp 153–4.

[43] Barry Rubin, *Revolution Until Victory? The Politics and History of the PLO* (Cambridge, Mass., 1994).

Chapter 8. Gunnar Jarring's Mission Impossible

[1] UN Document S/8247, 16 November 1967.

[2] GAOR, 1529th Plenary Meeting, 21 June 1967.

[3] U Thant, *View from the U.N.*, p 288.

4   UN Document S/8259, 23 November 1967.

5   This information about terms of reference is taken from Ambassador Gunnar Jarring's private papers, which the ambassador kindly gave me permission to study. They are deposited in the Swedish National Archives (*Riksarkivet*), but unfortunately have not been catalogued. They consist of loose pages collected together in folders. There is therefore no easy way of referring to them and I have used references to other sources where these are consistent with the Jarring papers.

6   Avi Shlaim, *The Iron Wall*, p 254.

7   *Ibid.*, pp 250–8.

8   PRO, FCO 17/36/12: Khartoum telegram No. 493 of 2 September 1967 to the Foreign Office.

9   Brian Urquhart, *A Life in Peace and War* (London, 1987), p 217.

10 UN document S 8309/Add. 1, 17 January 1968.

11 PRO, FCO 17/43/12: Cairo telegram No. 70 of 21 January 1968 to the Foreign Office.

12 Eban, *An Autobiography*, p 453.

13 PRO, FCO 17/43/23: Washington telegram No. 414 of 2 February 1968 to the Foreign Office.

14 PRO, FCO 17/43/24: UKMIS New York telegram No. 243 to the Foreign Office.

15 PRO, FCO 17/43/unnumbered: Foreign Office telegram No. 185 of 7 February 1968 to Tel Aviv.

16 PRO, FCO 17/43/42: Washington telegram No. 565 of 13 February 1968 to the Foreign Office.

17 PRO, FCO 17/43/47: Washington telegram No. 631 of 16 February 1968 to the Foreign Office.

18 PRO, FCO 17/43/45: Amman telegram No. 120 of 15 February 1968 to the Foreign Office.

19 PRO, FCO 17/43/40: Washington telegram No. 577 of 14 February 1968 to the Foreign Office.

20 PRO, FCO 17/43/57: Tel Aviv telegram No. 219 of 20 February 1968 to the Foreign Office.

21 PRO, FCO 17/43/60: Foreign Office telegram No. 748 to UKMIS New York; PRO, FCO 17/43/73: Washington telegram No. 699 of 24 February 1968 to the Foreign Office.

22 PRO, FCO 17/43/75: UKMIS New York telegram No. 466 of 26 February 1968 to the Foreign Office.

23 PRO, FCO 17/43/83: UKMIS New York telegram No. 499 of 28 February 1968 to the Foreign Office.

[24] PRO, FCO 17/43/86: UKMIS New York telegram No. 511 of 29 February 1968 to the Foreign Office.

[25] PRO, FCO 17/44/55: Foreign Office letter of 7 March 1968 to the Ministry of Defence.

[26] PRO, FCO 17/43/57: Tel Aviv telegram No. 219 of 20 February 1968 to the Foreign Office.

[27] PRO, FCO 17/44/89: Tel Aviv telegram No. 324 of 11 March 1968 to the Foreign Office.

[28] The lengthy correspondence about this proposal is in Jarring's private papers.

[29] UN Document S/8309/Add.2.

[30] PRO, FCO 17/44/11: Amman telegram No. 324 to the Foreign Office.

[31] U Thant, View from the U.N., pp 299–300.

[32] PRO, FCO 17/44/23 (sic): Amman telegram No. 443 of 6 May 1968 to the Foreign Office.

[33] PRO, FCO 17/45/148: UKMIS New York telegram No. 1332 of 20 May 1968 to the Foreign Office.

[34] The Americans passed on this information to their British colleagues. See PRO, FCO 17/45/172: Letter from Glass (New York) to Allen (Foreign Office).

[35] PRO, FCO 17/45/176: UKMIS New York telegram No. 1467 of 3 June 1968 to the Foreign Office.

[36] PRO, FCO 17/45/178: UKMIS New York telegram No. 1624 of 18 June 1968 to the Foreign Office.

[37] News of Jarring's meetings with Riad and Eban was conveyed to the Foreign Office by the Israeli Minister in London. See PRO, FCO 17/45/196: Foreign Office telegram No. 2978 of 2 July 1968 to UKMIS New York.

[38] Shlaim, The Iron Wall, p 226.

[39] Ibid., p 261.

[40] Ibid., p 262.

[41] PRO, FCO 17/45/204: Foreign Office telegram No. 3010 of 10 July 1968 to UKMIS New York.

[42] PRO, FCO 17/46/221: UKMIS New York telegram No. 1831 of 29 July 1968 to the Foreign Office.

[43] PRO, FCO 17/46/221: UKMIS New York telegram No. 1831 of 29 July 1968 to the Foreign Office.

[44] The whole process of exchanges of questions and answers is covered in PRO, FCO 17/89: Brief for the Foreign Secretary's Visit to New York for the General Assembly.

45 Published in *Public Papers of the Presidents of the United States: Lyndon B. Johnson, 1967–8*.

46 PRO, FCO 17/46/243: UKMIS New York telegram No. 2145 of 16 September 1968 to the Foreign Office.

47 PRO, FCO 17/46/253: UKMIS New York telegram No. 166 Saving of 26 September 1968 to the Foreign Office.

48 Shlaim, *The Iron Wall*, pp 262–3.

49 PRO, FCO 17/46/251: UKMIS New York telegram No. 2273 of 28 September 1968 to the Foreign Office.

50 PRO, FCO 17/88/49: UKMIS New York telegram No. 2440 of 10 October 1968 to the Foreign Office.

51 PRO, FCO 17/695/14: UKMIS New York telegram No. 2766 of 8 November 1968 to the Foreign Office.

52 Rafael, *Destination Peace*, p 199.

53 Eban, *An Autobiography*, p 454.

Chapter 9. Conclusion

1 Shlaim, *The Iron Wall*, p 236.

2 Brown, *In My Way*, pp 135–7.

3 Crossman, *The Diaries of a Cabinet Minister*, pp 352–65.

4 Brown, *In My Way*, p 135.

5 Wilson, *The Labour Government 1964–70*, pp 401–2.

6 Marcia Williams, *Inside No. 10* (London, 1972; abridged edition, 1975), p 159.

7 Shlaim, *The Iron Wall*, p 260.

8 Personal knowledge of author.

9 Parker (ed), *The Six-Day War*, p 200.

BIBLIOGRAPHY

Primary sources

UNITED NATIONS DOCUMENTS
A/3268 and A/3269, 3 November 1956
A/3302, 7 November 1956
A/3306 and A/3307, 7 November 1956
A/3375, 20 November 1956
A/6717, 13 June 1967
A/6669, 18 May 1967
A/6672, 18 May 1967
A/6730, 18 June 1967
GAOR, 1st Emergency Special Session, 562nd Meeting, 1 November 1956
GAOR, 665th, 666th and 667th Plenary Meetings, 1 March 1957
GAOR, 1529th Meeting, 21 June 1967
Resolution No. 181(II), 29 November 1947
Resolution No. 377(V), 3 November 1950
Resolution No. 997(ES-I), 2 November 1956
Resolution No. 1001(ES-I), 7 November 1956
Resolution No. 1125(XI), 2 February 1957
Resolution No. 2253 (ES-V), 4 July 1967
S/2322, 1 September 1951
S/3168/Add.1, 29 January 1954
S/3719, 29 October 1956
S/7896, 19 May 1967
S/8213, October 1967
S/8227, 7 November 1967
S/8229, 7 November 1967
S/8247, 16 November 1967
SCOR, 11th year, 751st meeting, 31 October 1956
SCOR, 1348th Meeting, 6 June 1967
SCOR, 1373rd Meeting, 9–10 November 1967

SCOR, 1375th Meeting, 13 November 1967

UK GOVERNMENT RECORDS
House of Commons Hansard, 6 June 1967
House of Commons Hansard, 7 June 1967
House of Commons Hansard, 24 January 1968
PRO, C(67)172, 31 October 1967
PRO, C.C.(67) 63rd Meeting, 2 November 1967
PRO, CAB 128/42 C(67) 31st, 32nd and 33rd Conclusions
PRO, FCO 17/36/various
PRO, FCO 17/43–45/various
PRO, FCO 17/88–89/various
PRO, FCO 17/434/various
PRO, FCO 17/493/1297
PRO, FCO 17/496/1499
PRO, FCO 17/695/various
PRO, FCO 28/406/28
PRO, FCO 39/170/1
PRO, FCO 39/191–2/various
PRO, FCO 39/265–7/various
PRO, FCO 39/269/various
PRO, PREM 13/1858, May 1967
PRO, PREM 13/1906, May/June 1967

US GOVERNMENT RECORDS
Foreign Relations of the United States 1955–57, vol. XVII: Arab–Israeli Dispute 1957 (Washington DC, 1990)
Foreign Relations of the United States 1964–68, vol. XVIII: Arab–Israeli Dispute 1964–67 (Internet)
Public Papers of the Presidents of the United States: Dwight D. Eisenhower 1956–7
Public Papers of the Presidents of the United States: Lyndon B. Johnson 1967–8
The Quest for Peace: Principal United States Public Statements and Related Documents on the Arab–Israeli Peace Process, 1967–83 (Washington DC, 1984)

ISRAELI GOVERNMENT RECORDS
Encyclopaedia Judaica
Israel's Foreign Relations: Selected Documents, 1947–1974, vols. 1 and 2

BBC MONITORING SERVICE
Summary of World Broadcasts, Second Series, Part 4, The Middle East and Africa, 1966–7 ME/2485/A/6, 6 June 1967; ME/2484/A/18, 7 June 1967; ME/2484/A/23, 7 June 1967

Secondary sources

MEMOIRS
Brown, George, *In My Way* (London, 1970 and 1971)
Bull, General Odd, *War and Peace in the Middle East: The Experience and Views of a U.N. Observer* (London, 1976)
Bullard, Reader, *The Camels Must Go: An Autobiography* (London, 1961)
Crossman, Richard, *Palestine Mission: A Personal Record* (London, 1947)
——, *The Diaries of a Cabinet Minister* (London, 1976), vol. 2
Dayan, Moshe, *Mappa Hadasha – Yahasim Aherim* (*New Map – Other Relations*) (Haifa, 1969)
——, *Story of My Life* (London, 1976)
Eban, Abba, *An Autobiography* (London, 1977)
——, *Personal Witness: Israel Through My Eyes* (New York, 1992)
Fawzi, Mahmoud, *Suez 1956: An Egyptian Perspective* (London, undated)
Fawzi, Muhammad, *Harb al-Thalatha Sanawat 1967–1970* (*The Three-Years War 1967–1970*) (Cairo, 1984)
Gore-Booth, Paul, *With Great Truth and Respect* (London, 1974)
Healey, Denis, *The Time of My Life* (London, 1989)
Hussein of Jordan, *My 'War' with Israel* (translated from the French) (London, 1969)
Johnson, Lyndon Baines, *The Vantage Point: Perspectives of the Presidency 1963–1969: A Personal Account* (New York, 1971)
Meir, Golda, *My Life* (London, 1975)
Nasser, Gamal Abd El-, *The Philosophy of the Revolution* (Cairo, undated)
Rabin, Yitzhak, *The Rabin Memoirs* (expanded edition, Berkeley, 1979)
Rafael, Gideon, *Destination Peace: Three Decades of Israeli Foreign Policy: A Personal Memoir* (London, 1981)
Rikhye, Major-General Indar Jit, *The Sinai Blunder* (London, 1980)
Rostow, Eugene V., *Peace in the Balance: The Future of American Foreign Policy* (New York, 1972)
Rusk, Dean, *As I Saw It* (New York, 1990)
Storrs, Ronald, *Zionism and Palestine* (London, 1940)
Tekoah, Yosef, *In the Face of Nations: Israel's Struggle for Peace* (New York, 1976)
U Thant, *View from the U.N.* (Newton Abbot, 1978)
Urquhart, Brian, *A Life in Peace and War* (London, 1987)

——, 'The United Nations in the Middle East: A 50-Year Retrospective', *Middle East Journal*, vol. 49, no. 4 (Autumn 1995)

Williams, Marcia, *Inside No. 10* (London, 1972; abridged edition, 1975)

Wilson, Harold, *The Labour Government 1964–1970: A Personal Record* (Tonbridge, 1971)

OTHER WORKS

Antonius, George, *The Arab Awakening* (London, 1938)

Bar-Zohar, Michael, *Ben Gurion*, translated by Peretz Kidron (London, 1978)

——, *Histoire Secrète de la Guerre d'Israël* (Paris, 1968)

Beckman, Morris, *The Jewish Brigade: An Army with Two Masters 1944–1945* (Staplehurst, 1998)

Black, Ian and Benny Morris, *Israel's Secret Wars: The Untold History of Israeli Intelligence* (London, 1991)

Brands, H.W., *The Wages of Globalism: Lyndon Johnson and the Limits of American Power* (New York, 1995)

Brecher, Michael, *Decisions in Israel's Foreign Policy* (London, 1974)

Bregman, Ahron and Jihan El-Tahri, *The Fifty Years War: Israel and the Arabs* (London, 1998)

Brenchley, Frank, *Britain and the Middle East: An Economic History 1945–1987* (London, 1989)

Brown, Judith M. and Wm. Roger Louis (eds) *The Oxford History of the British Empire, Volume IV. The Twentieth Century* (Oxford, 1999)

Burns, Lt-Gen E.L.M., *Between Arab and Israeli* (London, 1962)

Cattan, Henry, *Palestine, the Arabs and Israel* (London, 1969)

Christison, Kathleen, 'US Policy and the Palestinians, 1948–88', *Journal of Palestine Studies*, vol. XXVII, no. 3 (Spring 1998)

Churchill, Randolph S. and Winston S. Churchill, *The Six Day War* (London, 1967)

Clarke, Thurston, *By Blood and Fire: The Attack on the King David Hotel* (London, 1981)

Cohen, Avner, 'Cairo, Dimona and the June War', *Middle East Journal*, vol. 50, no. 2 (Spring 1996)

——, *Israel and the Bomb* (New York, 1998)

Cohen, Michael J. and Martin Kolinsky, *Demise of the British Empire in the Middle East* (Oxford, 1998)

Coles, John, *Making Foreign Policy: A Certain Idea of Britain* (London, 2000)

Copeland, Miles, *The Game of Nations: The Amorality of Power Politics* (London, 1969)

Craig, James, *Shemlan: A History of the Middle East Centre for Arab Studies* (Basingstoke, 1998)

Dann, Uriel, *King Hussein and the Challenge of Arab Radicalism: Jordan, 1955–1967* (Oxford, 1989)

—— (ed), *The Great Powers in the Middle East, 1919–1939* (New York, 1988)

Dickie, John, *Inside the Foreign Office* (London, 1992)

Dodd, C.H. and M.E. Sales, *Israel and the Arab World* (London, 1970)

Elpeleg, Zvi, *The Grand Mufti: Haj Amin Al-Hussaini: Founder of the Palestine Nationalist Movement* (London, 1993)

Gerges, Fawaz A., *The Superpowers and the Middle East: Regional and International Politics, 1955–1967* (Boulder, 1994)

Gilbert, Martin, *Israel: A History* (London, 1998)

Golan, Galia, *Soviet Policies in the Middle East from World War Two to Gorbachev* (Cambridge, 1990)

Grollenberg, Lucas, *Palestine Comes First* (London, 1980)

Haddad, William W., Ghada H. Talhami, and Janice J. Terry (eds), *The June 1967 War after Three Decades* (Washington DC, 1999)

Heikal, Mohammed Hassanein, *1967 – Al Infijar* (*1967 – The Eruption*) (Cairo, 1411 H.)

——, *Sphinx and Commissar: The Rise and Fall of Soviet Influence in the Middle East* (London, 1978)

——, *Secret Channels: The Inside Story of Arab–Israeli Peace Negotiations* (London, 1996)

Hourani, Albert H., *A History of the Arab Peoples* (London, 1991)

Hourani, Cecil, *An Unfinished Odyssey: Lebanon and Beyond* (London, 1984)

Kavanagh, Dennis and Anthony Seldon, *The Powers behind the Prime Minister: The Hidden Influence of Number Ten* (London, 1999)

Kayyali, A.W., *Palestine: A Modern History* (London, undated)

Kedourie, Elie, *England and the Middle East: The Destruction of the Ottoman Empire, 1914–1921* (Hassocks, 1956 and 1978)

——, *The Chatham House Version and Other Middle Eastern Studies* (London 1970, 1984)

Khouri, Fred J., *The Arab–Israeli Dilemma* (New York, 1968)

Kilani, Dr Haitham Al-, *Al-Istratijiyat Al-'Askariya Lil-Hurub Il-'Arabiya - Il-Isra'iliya, 1948–1988* (*Military Strategies of the Arab–Israeli Wars, 1948–1988*) (2nd edition, Beirut, 1991)

Korn, David A., *Stalemate: The War of Attrition and Great Power Diplomacy in the Middle East 1967–1970* (Boulder, 1992)

Kosuf, Hal (ed), *Israel and the Arabs: The June 1967 War* (New York, 1968)

Laqueur, Walter, *The Road to War 1967: The Origins of the Arab–Israel Conflict* (London, 1968)

Louis, Wm. Roger, *The British Empire in the Middle East 1945–1951* (New York, 1984)

Mansfield, Peter, *A History of the Middle East* (London, 1992)

Mitchell, Richard P., *The Society of the Muslim Brothers* (New York, 1969)

Monroe, Elizabeth, *Britain's Moment in the Middle East, 1914–1956* (London, 1963, revised 1981)

Morgan, Kenneth O., *Callaghan: A Life* (Oxford, 1997)

Mutawi, Samir A., *Jordan in the 1967 War* (Cambridge, 1987)

Neff, Donald, *Warriors for Jerusalem* (New York, 1984)

Nutting, Anthony, *Nasser* (London, 1972)

Parker, Richard B., *The Politics of Miscalculation in the Middle East* (Bloomington, 1993)

—— (ed), *The Six-Day War: A Retrospective* (Gainsville,1996)

Paterson, Peter, *Tired and Emotional: The Life of Lord George-Brown* (London, 1993)

Pedatzur, Reuven, 'Coming Back Full Circle: The Palestine Option in 1967', *Middle East Journal*, vol. 49, no. 2 (Spring 1995)

Quandt, William B., *Peace Process: American Diplomacy and the Arab–Israeli Conflict since 1967* (Washington DC, 1993)

Riad, Mahmoud, *The Struggle for Peace in the Middle East* (London, 1981)

Roth, Stephen J. (ed), *The Impact of the Six-Day War* (London, 1988)

Rubin, Barry, *Revolution Until Victory? The Politics and History of the PLO* (Cambridge, Mass., 1978)

Safran, Nadav, *From War to War: The Arab–Israeli Confrontation* (New York, 1969)

——, *Israel, The Embattled Ally* (Cambridge, Mass., 1978)

Said, Edward W., *Orientalism* (London, 1978)

Sela, Avraham, *The Decline of the Arab–Israeli Conflict: Middle East Politics and the Quest for Regional Order* (Albany, 1998)

Sharabi, Hisham, 'Interview with Lord Caradon', *Journal of Palestine Studies*, vol. V (1976)

Sherman, A.J., *Mandate Days: British Lives in Palestine 1918–1948* (London, 1997)

Shlaim, Avi, *War and Peace in the Middle East* (New York, 1994)

——, 'The Oslo Accord', *Journal of Palestine Studies*, vol. XXIII, no. 3 (1994)

——, *The Iron Wall: Israel and the Arab World* (New York, 2000)

Sykes, Christopher, *Cross Roads to Israel* (London, 1965)

Tessler, Mark, *A History of the Israeli–Palestinian Conflict* (Bloomington, 1994)

Vassiliev, Alexei, *Russian Policy in the Middle East: From Messianism to Pragmatism* (Reading, 1993)

Vital, David, *The Making of British Foreign Policy* (London, 1968)

Walker, Patrick Gordon, *The Cabinet* (2nd edition, London, 1970)

Wallace, William, *The Foreign Policy Process in Britain* (London, 1975)

Wasserstein, Bernard, *The British in Palestine* (Oxford, 1991)

Wilson, Harold, *The Chariot of Israel: Britain, America and the State of Israel* (London, 1981)

Yost, Charles W. 'The Arab–Israeli War: How It Began', *Foreign Affairs*, vol. 46, no. 2 (January 1968)

Zeinab, Abdel Latif M., *The United Nations Emergency Force, 1956–1967* (Stockholm, 1976)

NEWSPAPERS AND MAGAZINES
Daily Mail, 9 April 1970
Look, 4 March 1968
The Times, 19 May 1968

INTERVIEWS
Sir Richard Beaumont (British ambassador to Iraq in June 1967), London, 13 August 1998 and 15 July 1999

Lord Healey of Riddlesden (secretary of state for defence in 1967), London, 17 February 2000

Gerald Kaufman MP (personal link between the prime minister and the Israeli ambassador in London during the Six-Day War), London, 1 December 1999

Lord Thomson of Monifieth (minister of state in the Foreign Office in 1967), London, 1 September 1999

INDEX